## WEAVERS OF HOPE

# Una Familia Humana

# One Human Family

### JACK KERN

Published by Jack Kern Publishing
1011 Brodie Street, Unit 8
Austin, TX 78704

Copyright © 2011 Jack Kern

All rights reserved. This book, or parts thereof, may not be reproduced in any form without written permission of the publisher.

Printed in the United States of America

# Table of Contents

Acknowledgements . . . . . . . . . . . . . . . . . . . . . . . . . . . . . . . . . . . . . . . . . .1
Introduction . . . . . . . . . . . . . . . . . . . . . . . . . . . . . . . . . . . . . . . . . . . . . . .5
Map of Mexico showing Villa Garcia . . . . . . . . . . . . . . . . . . . . . . . . . . .7

**CHAPTERS**
Kiko and Rosalia. . . . . . . . . . . . . . . . . . . . . . . . . . . . . . . . . . . . . . . . . . .9
Jack. . . . . . . . . . . . . . . . . . . . . . . . . . . . . . . . . . . . . . . . . . . . . . . . . . . .35
Beginning Weavers of Hope . . . . . . . . . . . . . . . . . . . . . . . . . . . . . . . . .53
Fran . . . . . . . . . . . . . . . . . . . . . . . . . . . . . . . . . . . . . . . . . . . . . . . . . . .71
Maria . . . . . . . . . . . . . . . . . . . . . . . . . . . . . . . . . . . . . . . . . . . . . . . . . .91
Lupe . . . . . . . . . . . . . . . . . . . . . . . . . . . . . . . . . . . . . . . . . . . . . . . . . .107
Julieta . . . . . . . . . . . . . . . . . . . . . . . . . . . . . . . . . . . . . . . . . . . . . . . . .115
The Ripple Effect . . . . . . . . . . . . . . . . . . . . . . . . . . . . . . . . . . . . . . . .127
Visions and Dreams . . . . . . . . . . . . . . . . . . . . . . . . . . . . . . . . . . . . . .147

**APPENDICES**
Contact Information. . . . . . . . . . . . . . . . . . . . . . . . . . . . . . . . . . . . . .159
Student Sketches – by: Sr. Fran Smith. . . . . . . . . . . . . . . . . . . . . . . . .161
Student Letters . . . . . . . . . . . . . . . . . . . . . . . . . . . . . . . . . . . . . . . . . .169

# Acknowledgements

It takes a community of dedicated friends and supporters to get a book written and published. I feel truly blessed to have had such a nurturing and caring group of talented friends who have helped me. As the Eagles musical group sang about in the 1970s…"I get a peaceful, easy feeling" within me when I think about these wonderful people. Thanks to all of you, and to the many others who have supported me in so many ways.

In January of 2010, my sister-in-law and friend, Mary Warhol said to me, "Hey Jack, you should write a book about Weavers of Hope." I laughed in response to the idea.

Over the next week her suggestion kept coming back into my mind. I had been dreaming for several years about how we could take the work of Weavers of Hope to the next level, and expand the number of students and families that were being helped. The more I thought about it, the more it seemed reasonable to tell the story of the people of Villa Garcia and those people who are deeply immersed in the work. Because of that phone conversation with Mary, I began writing this book in early 2010.

Mary, a gifted writer and story teller, read the first chapter. She told me that it was good, and that gave me the confidence to keep going. I want to thank her for the inspiration, and the belief in me to tell the story. Her suggestions are an integral part of the book. I also thank her for her editing and patience with my many grammatical errors.

It's funny how things fall into place sometimes. I was working on a totally different project with Ken Steger. In our conversations it came out that he was a journalist who had extensive experience in writing, editing, and publishing. He also has a heart that cares deeply about others. We talked about the book, and he immediately offered to help.

Our morning bagel and coffee sessions have been both productive and fun. Ken's ideas and suggestions are all over this book. When he read the first chapter, he liked that it could almost stand alone as a short story. He encouraged me to think about writing a series of chapters that tell different stories about people's lives. He said that if those stories were interesting, it would be easy to weave them together and develop the overall manuscript. That was a wonderful insight, as were so many other suggestions from Ken.

What has been even better is the friendship that we have developed. Even though I have only known Ken for about a year, we have talked deeply about our lives, struggles, and spiritual journeys. What a blessing you are in my life, Ken.

I then began searching for a couple of readers who I could trust to give me honest feedback, both good and bad. Diann Broughton Hoops and Mary Beth Bigger were the two people that I knew would be the perfect choices. I have so much respect for both of them in so many ways. They both immediately said yes, and made me feel like they were honored to be asked. They have been with me chapter by chapter, and contributed countless ideas and suggestions to make the book better. Thank you, Diann and Mary Beth. I value you as friends and helpers on this project.

I also want to thank my friends Sean McGuire, Patrick Tourville, Terry Tourville, and Mike Richardson for doing a complete read of the entire manuscript during the final editing phase. Their insights and suggestions were most helpful in finalizing the text and getting it ready for publication.

My beloved wife, Martha, has been my partner, best friend, and supporter for 37 years now. Ken suggested that I have someone read the book to me and that I just sit back, close my eyes, and listen to how it sounds. There was no doubt in my mind that Martha would do this for me. Thank you, Martha, for everything, especially the hours of reading to me. That was so intimate and personal. I love you.

Sr. Fran Smith and Julieta are the two people who make Weavers of Hope so successful. They are in the field, and in daily relationships of solidarity with the people of Villa Garcia. They have documented factual information, conducted interviews, provided translations, and edited the manuscript. Without them, this book would not be possible. More importantly, without them this work would not be possible.

Thanks also to the countless others who have encouraged me and supported the work of Weavers of Hope. Each one of you is extremely important to me, probably more than you'll ever know.

Finally, thanks to my parents who loved me and supported me throughout their lives until their deaths in 1997. They were my first role models, even though I didn't know it at the time.

# Introduction

Hollywood has a great theme which they have been using in movies since the beginning of the motion picture industry. I call it the "underdog theme". You can probably name several movies right off the top of your head where the hero is bottoming out in life, then goes through this miraculous transformation and ends up achieving some great success. Rocky, Rudy, and the Pursuit of Happyness are three movies that always jump into my mind when I think about this theme.

For most of my life, I was able to go home from these movies, often a little teary-eyed, and then promptly forget about them. About 10 years ago all of that changed for me. I took an intensive, 30-week class on social justice issues in our world. It was called JustFaith. The underdogs from all over the globe took on real names and faces. I met some of them personally. Their stories and struggles became a part of me. For the first time in my life, I understood and felt the connection with all other people, my *una familia humana,* one human family.

For those of you who are parents, you know that when your children are in trouble and struggling, their issues become a part of your life. You want desperately to help them. This is what happened to me when I learned about the half of our world population that lives in poverty. I wanted to do something, however small it might be, to make a difference in some of their lives.

The big question was where to begin. God had an interesting way of helping me to answer that question. This book tells the story of how a group of us were given the opportunity to make a small difference in the world. The work of Weavers of Hope became a passion in my life from the very beginning. It was my way of helping one group of underdogs to position themselves for a shot at success.

For eight years Weavers of Hope has been slowly growing. The primary mission is to help Mexican students who live in poverty to continue their education. This gives them hope and a chance to succeed. Over half of the sponsored students in Weavers of Hope are in the university. The older students are in a position to make more of an immediate impact on their families and communities. It is happening.

Over 20 students from our program have now graduated from the university. They are finding meaningful work in Mexico, and helping their families. Many of them are sponsoring their younger siblings so that they, too, can continue in school. The graduates are positive role models for the younger students in the village.

Students who enter the program are required to maintain an overall 80% grade point average, help in the community, exchange letters with their sponsors, and actively participate in monthly meetings. They are being trained to become the leaders of the next generation. We are betting the future on them.

As of this writing Weavers of Hope has helped over 150 students in the village of Villa Garcia, Zacatecas, Mexico and the surrounding areas. Yet, the needs of this community and hundreds of others like them are enormous. As we observe the positive results, we can't help but wonder what can be done to expand the mission so that the organization can help many more deserving students.

People of all ages in the community are observing what is happening. Education is being seen as a real and tangible way to provide job opportunities. People are getting a vision of how you might be able to pull yourself out of poverty. The "underdog theme" is working in the lives of real people who are struggling.

My dream is that this book will inspire you in some way, and lead you toward a deeper connection with all of our brothers and sisters, both in the U.S. and internationally. Only in the depths of our hearts and in connection with our personal Higher Power will we know what is right for us. I will feel good about wherever that leads you. I feel wonderful about where it has led me.

# Map showing Villa Garcia

*"Something there is in me that struggles to be birthed,
kicks, pushes, tears
at what's between it and what's outside.
What it is that is to be birthed I do not know,
but it labors relentlessly.*

*And then for no apparent reason
its struggle seems to ease,
almost to the point of stillness,
but I know the labor continues."*

**from "TOBIY", Mike Richardson, ©2007**

# Kiko and Rosalia

It was a cold morning in February 2003. The well-dressed man stood on the predetermined street corner in Nuevo Laredo, Mexico at precisely 9 a.m. His presence projected an air of calm and self-confidence as he awaited the meeting with the group of nine Texans, whom he knew only by e-mail conversations. There was no doubt in his mind that the connections would be flawless and without undue surprises. He was accustomed to evaluating all the angles before arriving at a workable solution. He trusted his instincts and judgment, without any traces of arrogance.

Perhaps it was his extensive education, both in the classroom and in the world, that led to his demeanor. Perhaps it was the fact that he had lived in and visited multiple countries, unlike the majority of his fellow Mexican citizens. But it seemed to be more than all of that. He had great trust in his intellect, along with his judgment and analytical skills. He was also a man who was widely liked by people from many different cultures and from many different rungs on the economic ladder. He seemed equally at ease with all those he met, and his ease opened the door to new relationships.

He greeted our group of travelers as if he were the Mexican ambassador who was welcoming us to his country. Within a few minutes, all of us felt like we were in very capable hands. The members of our group who were most concerned about the safety issues of travel in Mexico breathed a collective sigh of relief. We all sensed that everything would be OK. Roberto, called Kiko by everyone, was clearly in charge of our destiny. We were all comfortable with that, as was Kiko.

He immediately embarked on establishing personal connections with each one of us, asking about our trip, our families, and our lives. He was content to listen as the nervous chatter spilled out of the talkers, and as the smiles and nods came out of the others. He smiled easily and listened carefully, as if each word was a treasured gem. He was an easy man to talk with. He gave you the sense that time had stopped, and that he was totally enthralled with this moment of personal encounter. In his mind the time for getting acquainted could linger indefinitely, until someone made a move to change it. But, he would not be the one to initiate change.

Eventually, as the initial greetings and dumping out of emotions were released, we decided to load back into our three cars and continue the journey into Mexico. Kiko was in the lead car with Mike and Sandra, the only married couple in our entourage. Sandra's close friend filled out their car. This group would get the first extended visit with Kiko. Later, we would all get our turn with him.

As we began to meander south from Nuevo Laredo through the state of Tamaulipas, Kiko let everyone else lead the conversations until they slowed down or ran out of immediate questions. When pauses occurred, he easily filled in the gaps with stories of Mexican history, culture, architecture, economics, life-styles, or personal information about his family. It was effortless on his part, like fitting simple, puzzle pieces together. He made you feel as if these new relationships had been in place for years.

Kiko talked about a simpler form of life in his village, which seemed like a throwback to times past. As he painted the picture, it was almost like looking at an old movie and observing how much life had changed by the twenty-first century. Homes without electricity, running water, or bathrooms were unimaginable to us. Many in his community washed by hand, wrung out their clothes manually, and hung them on clotheslines to dry. He spoke of donkeys loaded with firewood for cooking, as the cost of propane was too high for many. Our imaginations were having trouble envisioning the cultural differences which awaited us.

Kiko, whose English is limited, had an easy time in this first car, as all three of the Texans were totally fluent in Spanish. He would learn that Sandra was from Panama and her friend, Carmen, was from Cuba. Although the cultures of these three countries are different, they all have the commonality of being under the Latin umbrella. When Sandra "goes off" with verbal gusto, she always smiles and mentions that what we are observing is an integral part of the Latin culture. Things are done and communicated with passion. Kiko innately understood this. He grew up with it.

Later our team members would be deciding on the roles that each of us would play in Weavers of Hope, the name that we eventually gave to our organization. One of the first positions that we needed to fill was that of treasurer. Sandra, with her Latin roots in full swing, clearly let us know that she does not like numbers and mathematical things. However, when no one stepped up to take on that role, she pushed all of her strong feelings onto the back burner and volunteered to do it. She has been the only treasurer that Weavers of Hope has had for over eight years, and she has done the job with excellence and gusto.

Sandra, Mike, and their two children, Caroline and John Michael, make up a truly top notch family. Caroline has the caring heart of her parents. Her study abroad program in Japan broadened her already wide vision of our global connections.

As a recent university graduate, Caroline is intellectually gifted, socially motivated, and endlessly fascinated with learning and helping others. She is a well-respected and emulated leader among her peers. Sandra reminds her often of the responsibilities that leaders need to accept. Usually, she responds positively to these gentle challenges from her mother.

John Michael is athletic, spiritual, and wise beyond his years. He demonstrates amazing maturity for a young boy in middle school. He, too, is a leader among his peers. He has a beautiful relationship with his friends and with each member of his family, especially with his dad, Mike. Seeing them together, throwing a football or talking, tells you the whole story of their relationship without the need for words. It is obvious.

Kiko, too, had an especially close relationship with his only son, Roberto (Beto). He and Mike talked openly and honestly about the special feelings that existed with their only sons. The sons were the last born in both families. Yet, both fathers also talked with love and pride about their daughters.

Kiko and Rosalia's older daughter, Estefania (Fany), has the best qualities of both of her parents. She is a high achiever in school, friendly, popular, and noticeably motivated. People knew that she would be successful. Ariana, the younger daughter, is quieter by nature, but also quite talented. She was on the internet often, and was teaching herself English. Beto, their son, is a little Kiko in looks and mannerisms.

As we continued driving, Kiko told us that few people or schools had phones. This meant that the schools operated without internet access, a fact that was hard to imagine. Computer skills were one of the many things that Kiko's three children were learning at home.

The conversation continued to meander quite naturally over a wide range of topics.

As we drove farther into the center of the country the landscape changed. Joshua trees and prickly pear cactus lined the highway in number and size that were mesmerizing. They stretched out into the arid desert as far as the eye could see.

Food stands improvised from plywood, concrete blocks, and lamina seemed to pop up in even the most remote locations. Occasional settlements appeared with a cluster of makeshift homes grouped together. Then, it was back to unending miles of rugged terrain and scorched deserts. The blue skies were interrupted only by soft white clouds hanging gently overhead.

An occasional PEMEX (Petroleum of Mexico) gas station would be strategically positioned along the highway. The state-owned petroleum company was the tenth largest in the world. It was nationalized in 1938 under the leadership of President Lazaro Cardenas, a name that shows up on various street signs and buildings throughout Mexico.

Kiko avoided the *autopistas,* toll roads, in an attempt to be respectful of our travel budget. The free roads were good enough for him. We dodged pot holes and went over endless *topes,* speed bumps. The travel was further complicated by countless old cars and trucks that were putting along at painfully slow speeds. We needed to coordinate our passing so that all three cars in our caravan could get around the slow moving vehicles before accelerating to a normal speed. Within a matter of minutes, we were usually stalled behind another old clunker, and it was time to repeat the passing ritual.

The slow pace was tiring, but the real challenge came in the city of Monterrey, the third largest metropolitan area in Mexico. Sometimes called the "Pittsburgh of Mexico", Monterrey is a major producer of steel, iron, cement, glass, and many other products. The factories churn constantly, filling the air with contamination, which is often trapped by the surrounding mountain ranges. The poor air quality is unmistakable, even to the naked eye. Almost four million inhabitants crowd the streets with cars and trucks which add their own toxins to the air. The Los Angeles air looks pure in comparison.

All of this was distressing enough, but trying to navigate the city and its traffic with our three-car caravan was virtually impossible. Inevitably, two of our cars would get through a crowded intersection, leaving one stranded at a red light. The leaders would need to look for a safe place to pull over and wait for the car that didn't make it through. Horns were blaring, curses were shouted, and wild hand gestures gave the appearance of a conductor gone insane. The people of Mexico are generally gentle and patient, until they get behind the wheel of a car. Then it is a Jekyll and Hyde transformation.

Such it was going through Monterrey. In the summer time you can do all of this lovely navigating in temperatures that exceed 100 degrees Fahrenheit. Thank God it was February!

When we finally emerged from the south side of the city, most of us were wrung out, exhausted, and frustrated. We were functioning on little sleep and had been in the cars for about 12 hours at this point. We would later learn that the *autopista* bypassed Monterrey. For a small fee, one could avoid these horrors, maintain sanity, and not have to breathe the toxic air. The tolls began to look like a real bargain.

Kiko was unfazed by all of this, maintaining his sense of calm in the midst of the chaos. Economic conditions have forced him, and many other Mexican citizens, to forego the luxury of paying the tolls and travelling in relative ease. He has learned to gut it out in many aspects of his life, as have his fellow citizens. Driving on the free roads, and accepting whatever inconveniences come with the territory, is just a part of life.

As we pushed on, exhaustion set in for me, and I crashed in the back seat when my turn to drive was over. Many of the others seemed to be doing OK, and Kiko was still chattering away and smiling, seemingly oblivious to the inconveniences. You got the impression that he could have continued in this mode for quite some time. The goal of reaching Villa Garcia, Zacatecas was set, and he was determined to reach that goal, with us safely intact. What is even more noteworthy is that he seemed to be enjoying the trip. I realized what a wimp I can be, especially when I get tired.

In the years leading up to year 2000 and the turn of the millennium, I had been truly enjoying not having a paying job for the first time in 25 years. My work as a computer software person was solid, well paying, and reasonably interesting. The people I worked with were really good folks, and the management staff was fair and ethical. But it was not my dream job, not something that made me want to get out of bed in the morning.

If I had known what my dream job was and been willing to look at earning considerably less income, perhaps I would have changed careers. But that was not in the cards. I didn't really know what I wanted to do, and I got more comfortable each year as I saw the balance in my investment accounts growing and could anticipate an early retirement.

The fact that my wife, Martha, did the same work as I did, allowed us to dream about and plan for a really early retirement. The official term was actually not retirement, but quitting, because it would be several years before our modest pensions would kick in. Nonetheless, after 25 years in the profession, we felt like it was retirement. We both dreamed of life after our full time, corporate jobs.

Initially I felt like I was on vacation rather than retired. Subconsciously it felt like I would be returning to work after vacation. But as the vacation extended, I slowly realized that I had entered a new phase of life, one which was exciting and also unknown. Being able to shed the corporate chains created an awful lot of free time for the first time in my life. I had gone from Louisiana State University (LSU) directly into my job and family life, so time had been scarce for many years. Now time would be abundant.

In the programming environment we were trained to develop our analytical, left-brained skills. As a result of this training, I would sit down and think about all of the things that I might want to do with the second half of my life. I made lists of the possibilities. There were strong feelings of excitement about the upcoming freedom. My health and energy levels were top notch. I couldn't wait. It felt like a kid being turned loose in a toy store and being told that you can get pretty much whatever you want. Where to begin?

The first big change was moving from Houston, where I worked, to Austin. I had grown up in New Orleans, a city with a rich and interesting tradition, but also with strong currents of deeply imbedded racism. It was a segregated city, although not formally so. With ridiculously low property taxes, there was little money to fund the public school system.

What developed from that situation was its own form of segregation. Private schools were the escape hatch for many white kids, whose parents could afford to send them to these schools. The ripple effect was predictable. The private schools were well funded, could attract the best teachers, and were clearly college preparatory focused. The graduates from these schools were expected to go on to the university, and almost all of them did. They got good jobs and continued the cycle with their children.

The poorer kids, largely African American, had to survive in the public high schools, with less of everything. This unequal playing field still exists in New Orleans today. In 2005, hurricane Katrina made these ugly realities more visible on the national stage.

New energy flowed into all of us as Kiko pointed out the sign showing that we had entered Villa Garcia, almost 20 hours after leaving Austin, Texas. As we pulled up to Kiko's home, his three children were out front to greet us, abuzz with energy. His wife, Rosalia, stood with Fran, keeping an eye on the kids.

Fran would be the cornerstone for the work that would eventually become Weavers of Hope. She had been living in the village for several years, and was a well-accepted member of the community. Weavers of Hope would eventually make her name known throughout Villa Garcia, and in many of the surrounding areas.

Standing quietly in the background were representatives from all of our host families. They smiled and greeted us, while studying our faces carefully. They were as curious about us as we were about them. We thanked Kiko for his leadership and patience and said goodnight to everyone. We were then escorted back to the homes of our host families, where we would spend the next four nights.

One of the biggest logistical decisions was how to house everyone in Villa Garcia, since there are no hotels or inns. In planning our accommodations, Fran, Kiko, and Rosalia had to juggle a variety of factors. The biggest challenge was in finding space in already overcrowded homes. Other obstacles included finding reliable host families, covering the translation needs, and being sure that purified water was available for drinking and food preparation. Drinking the tap water in Mexico is not recommended for visitors, as it often causes dysentery.

Most of the logistical juggling was accomplished by Fran, Kiko, and Rosalia in conjunction with the host families. These three also had the job of arranging our schedule, deciding who we should talk with, and covering all of our general needs. We were a group of people from many backgrounds and comfort levels. They decided that the best approach would be to work with the families with whom they had the strongest connections in Villa Garcia, and who could make a room available for four nights.

For the most part we were assigned two to a home, with at least one person who spoke a decent level of Spanish. I was the only exception to this rule for a couple of reasons. I was the only male other than Mike, Sandra's husband. Secondly, I had almost no worries or concerns about any aspect of this trip, including the fact that my Spanish was not all that good. So, it was decided that I would stay solo in the home of Abel, Consuelo, Maria, and the rest of their children. This would turn out to be a very special family for me, one whose home I would visit on all of my future trips to Villa Garcia.

The Spanish language has a term called *media naranja,* literally, the other half of my orange. What it really means is that your *media naranja* is the one person in the universe who completes your soul…soul mate in English. Rosalia is Kiko's *media naranja.*

To stay with the food analogies, Rosalia fills the holes in the Swiss cheese of Kiko's personality. Kiko leans hard in the direction of being a workaholic, totally focused, and driven to succeed. His intensity almost manifests itself as visible beams of light as he concentrates all of his energy on a task. He pushes himself hard.

Rosalia's eyes sparkle and her smile widens when she mischievously breaks his energy field. She is like the wise coach of a sports team who knows when to call a timeout to break the other team's momentum. She serves up exactly the change of pace that he needs to keep his head from exploding in over-concentration.

Rosalia is a diversified woman, fun and playful on the one hand, and tremendously capable on the other. She is the bookkeeper and accountant for their small business, the mother of three talented children, and Kiko's true partner. She has also managed to squeeze in a few business classes at the university. Her job description doesn't allow for a lot of free time. Yet, she has the easiness of demeanor that you would expect from someone with a much slower schedule.

She often invited me to sit down in her tiny kitchen while she was preparing a meal. She loved the social dimensions of being with others and talking. Rosalia is also an outstanding cook, for which I am as grateful as Kiko, runs a small cake decorating venture, and is an active member in a couple of groups which do social outreach work in their community. Like Kiko, she doesn't seem to have any limitations.

Rosalia grew up in a large family in the city of Aguascalientes, about an hour drive from Villa Garcia. While attending the university, she met Kiko's sister, who introduced the couple. The rest happened very quickly.

Kiko and Rosalia were married, and moved into Kiko's family home in Villa Garcia. Their bedroom was the very same room where Kiko was born 30 years earlier with the help of a local midwife. Fany, their first born child, entered the world a couple of years later, and their next generation was begun.

Kiko and Rosalia told numerous stories about the history of Villa Garcia, what life was like, and the desperation of many of the local people. They told us that the local diet was very simple. Beans, rice, tortillas, eggs, locally made cheese, and nopalitos from the abundant cactus plants were their staples. There is a high incidence of physical and mental deformities in Villa Garcia that many attribute to the lack of a balanced diet and contaminated water.

Kiko and Rosalia also talked openly and freely about their own family and friends. Their rock-solid values were apparent. Their three children, Fany, Ariana, and Beto, flowed in and out of the rooms delighting all of us with their openness and smiles. Before meals, they carried plates, utensils, and tortillas to the table to accompany the feast that Rosalia was casually laying out before us.

Rosalia's ease and grace in handling a variety of tasks at the same time amazed me. She would be cooking, directing the kids, engaged in a conversation with us, and able to deal with the special needs for attention that three young children have. None of this multi-tasking bothered her in the least. The kids were three engaging children – playful, intelligent, and physically beautiful. Their parents proudly showed them off to their visitors from Austin, and the kids did not disappoint them.

Over the years, I have spent a significant amount of time at the home and office of Kiko and Rosalia. As I observed their interactions with the people who trickled through their office it was clear that they were community leaders in Villa Garcia, known and liked by almost everyone. Their little internet and photocopy business in the center of town attracted an almost constant flow of customers, some just stopping in to say hello or exchange a story. The nine computers were often filled, mostly with young people. The information super highway is flourishing, even in selected spots in Villa Garcia.

I thought of how the internet has connected our global community. Instant news, jokes, and messages are just seconds away from even the most remote locations. Since few people can afford personal computers in the village, Kiko's cafe does pretty well. However, the costs of the hardware and being connected to the internet are significant.

While keeping a watchful eye on the internet business, Kiko would often be deeply engaged in conversations with local *campesinos,* farmers. They would be poring over paperwork, which looked to be tedious. Kiko, as he was with us, was calm and patient as he explained things to the *campesinos.* I wondered what all of this was about.

When there was a pause in the action, Kiko sat me down at his desk, pulled out a paper and pencil, and described another one of his business ventures.

Over the years, I would learn of many more entrepreneurial undertakings that he was dreaming up. He seemed to have an endless number of ideas to go along with his endless supply of energy. His mind lived in over-drive.

This particular venture with the farmers was to help them obtain small loans which would support their farming business. Through connections with a large financial institution, Kiko was a kind of middleman in the process. He interviewed the *campesinos,* processed their loans, and collected their monthly payments. Typically, they used the borrowed money for feed for the animals, fertilizer, seeds, or some other basic raw material. Then when their crops were harvested, they were able to repay their loans. I asked about defaults on loans, thinking that they would be frequent. That was not the case. There were few defaults because the *campesinos* often used their livestock as collateral. They were not about to receive more capital than they could repay. Their livestock was essential to their survival.

Kiko is an extremely good businessman. He is also a businessman with a social conscience, always insuring that the interest rates are fair, based on the local standards. The truth is that Kiko is good at a tremendous number of things. What he doesn't know, he researches, studies, and learns. He seems to remember everything. Then he uses that foundational knowledge to add more depth to his mastery of the subject.

Kiko had never been directly involved in the construction business until he built Fran's little brick home in the country, about two miles from the village. He learned as he went, doing some tasks himself, and subcontracting others. The final product was outstanding, simple in design, functional, and perfectly suited to Fran.

A few years later, he would supervise the construction of a large hospitality center and his family home. He would continue to do many of the tasks himself. Occasionally, he would ask me to buy specialty tools or materials in the United States, and bring them on my next trip to Villa Garcia. He would always have exact specifications, including websites and model numbers to make sure that his communications were precise. His attention to detail was noteworthy, and much appreciated. I never had to return anything due to lack of specifications from him. His family home and the hospitality center would be separated from Fran's home by a short distance. The three buildings evolved into their own little compound.

Fran's house sits about a football field's distance off the road. The long driveway that leads to her quaint home is lined with large maguey plants. The surface of the driveway is covered with rocks which are readily available in the surrounding hills. Since the cost of labor is frightfully low, it is most economical to build driveways in this manner.

Kiko and Rosalia's larger home was to the right of Fran's house. It had red window frames which brilliantly stood out against the soft browns and pronounced greens of the surrounding landscape. A well-constructed and visually appealing outhouse stood between the two homes, although both had indoor plumbing and flush toilets. It served as a backup when there was an interruption in the water services, which was somewhat frequent.

Across the street was the hospitality center which was built over eight years, as funds became available. It was a large white structure with the same red window frames as Kiko's house. The sign on the wall read Casa Clemens, in memory of Fran's deceased father. Much of the cost of construction was covered by the inheritance which Fran received from her dad. Casa Clemens would host various meetings, retreats, and other large gatherings. Visitors to Villa Garcia would eventually be able to stay there.

Fran met Kiko and Rosalia while they were living in Florida at the home of Kiko's sister. Kiko was working on an advanced degree at the university. When he finished the degree, he and Rosalia invited Fran to visit Mexico. They hoped that she would consider it as a possibility for her home.

Kiko also hoped that Fran might be able to help find markets for the weavers and other artisans of his village. Kiko's father, like many in his village, had been a weaver who passed on the trade to his son. Villa Garcia is a village that has been weaving for hundreds of years. In the later 1900s, cheap labor in countries like China and the Philippines had significantly cut into their marketing distribution network. Other artisans who produced wood and stone carvings, dream catchers, embroidery, crocheting, knitting, and cross stitching had even fewer outlets for their wares.

Many of the artisans were forced to take low-paying factory jobs in the nearby city of Aguascalientes. A typical salary would be about $45 U.S. for a week's work. The work was hard, and over two hours was spent commuting on the buses each day. The work days were long. The cost of the bus transportation cut deeper into their meager pay.

Often, the jobs required being on your feet all day. Breaks were scarce and short. Sometimes workers had to wait for a break to use the bathroom. The grueling conditions often excluded older adults from the workforce. They were forced to depend on family support or begging, as there was no such thing as social security or medicare.

As the phases of Kiko's life were slowly revealed, one had to wonder where the limits of this man were. In fact, you almost wondered if there were any limits. He and Rosalia made a quite formidable team. Their three young children seemed to have been genetically blessed with many gifts from their parents. These gifts were supplemented by an environment that nurtured learning of all forms, and taught responsibility.

When my wife, Martha, first saw Kiko's picture she commented that he was *guapo,* very handsome. As I described all of his other qualities, she listened in amazement. Kiko had exactly the right skills to earn a very healthy income in the business world. I admired him for choosing to work and live in Villa Garcia, with an eye out for helping his fellow community members. He and Rosalia, along with Fran, have done an enormous amount of good in their village.

After graduating from LSU, I moved to Houston to begin the working phase of my life. My time in Houston was largely focused on family and work. There was not time for much else.

Houston's climate was much like New Orleans, hot and humid, with long summers, mild winters, and short springs and autumns. The city was vibrant, culturally diverse, and had connections to a wide range of activities, including sports and the arts. The racism that I grew up with in New Orleans was not so noticeable in Houston. Most of the people I worked with were from other cities and states. They were open to forming friendships, so it was easy to break in. Having two children also connected us immediately to other young families in our neighborhood.

The early years of corporate freedom found me slowly transitioning into a life that included more service projects. There was sort of a gentle urge within me that wanted to give something back to other people and to the community. I tried several projects of various types to see what felt best. I've often enjoyed jumping in and learning by experience. Why take sailing lessons when you can hop in a boat, see how the wind hits the sails, and watch what happens?

I guess it's a bit of impatience in me. But, I think it goes farther than that. I feel like I could analyze things forever without really knowing how they feel until I try them out for size. In the programming world they had a special name for these "jumping in" projects. They were called prototypes. I always wondered if the official sounding name was just a way to make you feel better while you jumped in and avoided much of the tedium of detailed analysis. Regardless, this philosophy worked for me.

Anyway, good or bad, that was my approach to service projects. My experiences revealed a fairly consistent outcome. The projects that I was trying out just didn't generate much excitement and passion. This is not to say that there was no sense of satisfaction, because there was. But the real energy and joy were missing. It was more like going through the motions, trying to do something worthwhile, and being left largely unfulfilled. Yet, being an optimist, I felt like I would eventually find the right type of projects to work on. Most of the other parts of my life felt very good. I just needed to balance it out a little with some meaningful work.

Somewhere in the middle of this searching, I stumbled onto something which struck the chord I had been waiting for, so much so that it startled me. Learning Spanish never made it on to any of the daydream lists that I made a few years earlier. However, when I began taking Spanish classes, they grabbed my attention and focus in an almost compelling way.

Martha and I took a conversational Spanish class with some friends, before travelling to Mexico. All four of us really enjoyed it, and liked the idea of being able to travel in Mexico with a few, ordinary words which would be useful. We felt like it would help us to navigate the country and be friendly to those we met. The class was adding a pleasant, new dimension to the pre-trip planning.

When we finished the course, I was already hooked. I thought it would be fun to take another step and do the conversational II Spanish class. Martha and the other couple had different ideas. They thought that one class was plenty, and I let go of my thoughts about continuing on with Spanish, at least for the time being.

Nevertheless, I couldn't wait to try out my new "travel" vocabulary with the Mexican citizens. As it turned out, they often didn't understand me, but it didn't seem to matter much to me. I kept trying. I am usually not an extrovert, but I was relentless on continuing to try to communicate with each person who crossed our path on the trip. The fact that I was trying seemed to generally please them, and that was enough to keep me going.

Another event that influenced learning Spanish was precipitated by our daughter, Kennedy. After her freshman year at the University of Texas, she decided to do a summer study abroad program at the University of Salamanca in Spain. My 25-year-old son, Josh, and I went to meet Kennedy at the end of her classes. The three of us and three of Kennedy's Spanish language classmates travelled together in Spain for a couple of weeks.

That experience truly stoked the embers for taking more formal language classes. When we returned to Austin, I enrolled to take Spanish at Austin

Community College. Learning the language became my hobby and my passion. It provided me with the buzz of excitement that was missing in my other work projects.

I conjugated verbs in my head as I swam my morning laps at the community pool. Figuring out how to say things in Spanish became my Sudoku. *Primer Impacto,* First Impact, was the program on Spanish television that was my regular listening lab. I would often laugh at myself when I thought about what my student years at LSU could have been had I put that much effort into learning.

The fascination of learning Spanish soon got mixed in with my love for travelling, and that combination was dynamite. Travelling had always been almost obsessive with me. When I was young, my family always took a week of vacation each year, even though my parents had to scrape and save all year to be able to do it.

We would get literature on where we were going. Mom, Dad, and I would pore over maps, and dream about the adventures that would be there. As a young, impressionable child, I created a fantasyland in my head. Wherever we were going became magical to me. The roots for the desire to travel were growing, and they only got stronger over the years.

When I learned of the possibility of going to Spanish speaking countries to take special immersion classes, I felt like I had hit the mother lode. The idea of combining travel, culture, learning, meeting local people, and adventure, was almost too good to be true. The Spanish immersion programs provided all of those benefits, plus they existed in many different countries and cultures.

There was nothing to hold back my imagination. I visualized spending time in these strange, foreign lands. Part of my formal language classes covered various country profiles and places of interest. This fed into my dreams. All of it was quite alluring, and my mind raced with the possibilities.

When I enrolled in my first Spanish immersion class, I was excited and a little nervous. It was in Ensenada, Mexico, about 2 hours south of San Diego, on the Pacific coast. The location and climate were perfect, and Kennedy decided that she would do it with me. That seemed like a tremendous father-daughter thing to do, as she was also fascinated with the language.

We stayed with a lovely family who spoke to us only in Spanish. They were able to adjust the level of conversation to wherever we were on the learning scale. Diana, the mom, was an outgoing friendly person that loved to have us in the kitchen while she was cooking. She was curious about our lives and ready to tell us about hers.

Her kitchen was bright and friendly with sunlight flowing through the windows, and a backdrop of green space beyond the windows. The floors and counter tops were covered in colorful tiles with paintings of vines and flowers adorning the perimeter. Her cooking pots hung from a large rack over the island counter.

It felt good to sit at the kitchen bar and talk with Diana while she puttered away preparing the meal. Mexican music played softly in the background, and various people wandered in and out while we were talking. I learned that her parents and various other family members all lived on this same little alleyway. They flowed in and out of each other's homes and lives comfortably and with little fanfare. It was a different connection to family than what I knew.

The time that we spent gathered around the dining room table with the family felt very normal, not like we were guests. They included us in some of the conversation and at other times went on with their family communications, not having to worry about us understanding. When they were interacting among themselves, it gave us a chance to listen. We could also drift off if our minds needed to rest from the rigors of conversing in a new language. That was a nice break.

My bedroom was a small, simple single. As I lay in bed, I could look out of the window at a vibrant, coral bougainvillea spreading its flowering leaves over an adobe wall. It was surrounded by rich green plants and trees. When the sunlight hit the brightly colored leaves they lit up as if there were light bulbs illuminating them. It was an idyllic setting. The bougainvillea shrubs flourished in that climate and created a sensual feast for the eyes throughout the streets of Ensenada.

Classes were from 9 a.m. to 1 p.m., giving us time to walk home for the big meal, which is typically served in mid afternoon, and followed by a siesta, or quiet time. Many workers would then return to work after the midday break and work until 8 or 9 p.m., sometimes later.

Kennedy was in a more advanced group than I was, but we were able to walk to school together, take breaks at the same time, and then have time after lunch to be tourists. One of Diana's younger sisters, who lived in the family alleyway, invited us to hear her sing in a local club called *La Tortuga*, The Turtle, on Friday night. When Kennedy and I walked into the club, she came over immediately to welcome us. We felt special.

Another night, a group of us from class went to the local karaoke bar and had a really good time drinking Negra Modelo, my favorite beer, and urging one another to take a turn at the mike, which I did not do. And so the trip went for two wonderful weeks. My Spanish was being moved along nicely, and the cultural experiences were delightful and enriching.

Another immersion class experience was in San Juan, Puerto Rico. My close friends, Gordon and Susan, also liked to play around with learning Spanish. The three of us got really excited as we planned our adventure to San Juan to study Spanish and explore the city.

We stayed with Zori, who taught in one of the universities in San Juan. She was a young, vivacious lady with a special interest in music, dance, and the arts. She introduced us to her friends and spent a couple of nights taking us around the city. One night a week, the art galleries and shops in Old Town stay open later, and serve wine and cheese or other snacks. As Zori led us to some of her favorite places, we were carried away by the sights, sounds, and smells which added their charm to the historic district.

Another night, she took us to a special music venue down close to the water. The open air sides were covered by a thatched roof, and the mixture of ocean breezes and salsa music filled the air. It was a place where the locals went, and Zori was obviously a person who many people knew and liked. She was our passport to acceptance into their culture.

Old San Juan, on the northern shore of Puerto Rico, overlooks the Atlantic Ocean from atop the highest point in the city. Quincentennial Plaza, the hub of some of the most significant structures from Colonial times, was constructed in 1992-1993 to celebrate the 500th anniversary of the discovery of the New World. A monumental, totemic sculpture in black granite and ceramics rises from the plaza's top level. Clear and sweeping views from the plaza extend to the El Morro Fortress, constructed in 1540, which was built to guard San Juan Bay.

San Juan was a magical place to explore. Zori helped to bring it alive for us. The language school was also excellent, continuing to stretch my abilities in Spanish. It was a wonderful week in Puerto Rico.

Over the next couple of years there were other Spanish immersion classes in Antigua, Guatemala, and San Miguel de Allende, Mexico which were also very special times. These immersion classes supplemented my training in the formal, university classes and brought another dimension to the learning process which was fascinating. I had no clue that learning Spanish was going to play out in strange new ways in the near future. For now, it was just plain fun. Spanish was in my heart before my heart was fully with the Latin American people. That was soon to change.

On that first trip to the village of Villa Garcia, the days were cram packed with meeting people, talking, seeing the village, and trying to process all of the information. Abel, Consuelo, Maria, and their family gave me a solid, secure home base from which to operate. It was also nice to know that I would get to return to them in the evenings for a meal and some time to relax within the warm kindness of their family home.

The hilly, picturesque town of Villa Garcia, with about 8,000 residents, is located in the geographic center of Mexico. Its humble charm is accentuated by brightly painted buildings and homes. Lively music blares from many of the small businesses, and the shouts and banter of the residents fill the air.

We received a few unwelcoming stares, but many more smiles and nods, along with the friendly greeting of *buenos dias,* good morning. Almost every block contains little family-run stores with everything from basic groceries to freshly cooked food. Rotisseries with colorful, well-seasoned chickens and meats send out smells which make your mouth water. It is a constant feast for the senses.

Sandra and Mike stayed with Don Chuy and Socorro in a simple home with exquisite grounds, flowers, gardens, and Don Chuy's rudimentary wood-working tools. He carved intricate, detailed masks and faces from balsa wood with these basic tools. During the visit, he would give all of us a demonstration of how his faces emerged from a raw chunk of wood. Part of our leaving package included the mask of our choosing. This was no small gift for a hard-working artisan, but it was one that he gave with pleasure. It was another testimony to the bountiful generosity of these humble people.

Don Chuy and Socorro lived largely off of their land. They tended to the farm animals, worked the gardens, grew fruit trees, made their own wine, and seemed to relish in each other's company after forty plus years of marriage. They led us on a tour of their land, some 50 acres, explaining how things were used and cared for, answering questions, and proudly letting us experience a glimpse of their traditional Mexican lives. One of the gems of the tour was a concrete bed frame rising in a perfect rectangle off the bedroom floor. When covered properly with a mattress, they assured us that it was quite comfortable, also providing a refreshing level of cool in the summer months.

Pictures of their children and grandchildren lined the walls of their modest little home. They told stories of their family history. The sparkle in their eyes readily revealed that family meant everything to them. A friendship formed quickly between the two couples. Sandra and Mike often talk of Don Chuy and Socorro.

Each day had a full itinerary of people to meet and activities. One day, the entire group came to Abel and Consuelo's home, which I now thought of as "my home". Abel explained the brick making process in full detail, with animated demonstrations. Consuelo proudly exhibited her completed needlework projects, and answered an array of questions about the materials, patterns, uses, and potential for sales.

We strolled through their gardens, looking at their sheep, goats, flowering plants, vegetables and fruits. In the distance, a donkey was pulling a plow through a field, in preparation for sowing. It felt like a time warp. Seeing the donkey and plow in place of a John Deere tractor felt like a flashback to ages past. Life was simpler and slower here.

Abel and Consuelo's land, like Don Chuy's, had a magical feel to it. The pastels of the sky and hills basking in the bright sunshine, along with the slower pace of life had a calming effect on me. I closed my eyes, took a deep breath, and released a lot of the clutter. My mind felt peaceful and composed here. After only 2 days, I felt a sense of belonging. Being accepted into Abel and Consuelo's home and family was a large part of feeling so comfortable. I mentally thanked them for being so welcoming.

On another day, our entire group was taken to the site of the collapse of the earthen dam. We got to stand in the gaping hole where the wall caved in and where the waters from the reservoir started their descent into an unsuspecting village. Kiko told stories of the disaster. Everything seemed more real to us as we stood at the site of the breach and talked about the events of that morning in the summer of 2002.

Standing there in the bottom of the U-shaped terrain, I got a sense of the amount of water that went through that hole. It was approximately 40 feet to the tops of the U on each side, and about 200 feet wide. I felt extremely small and deeply touched as I stood in that hole in the earth and looked up, imagining what had happened.

Each home we visited, along with our host families, rolled out the red carpet and gave us the best they had in terms of themselves, their stories, their food, and their attention. We were treated as honored guests. I imagined that this might be how a head of state felt when visiting a foreign country. I thought about how my own personal acceptance and hospitality was lacking compared to what I was receiving. This was one of many things that I learned from the people of Villa Garcia, and it was a good lesson for me to take in and ponder.

Fran quietly orchestrated our schedules, like a conductor calling out her musicians at just the right moment. She was a part of everything that we did, involved in all of the conversations, translating things as needed, and looking to be sure that everyone was doing OK. It was a quiet, gentle, motherly, watchful love that she gave us. At just the right times, she wisely interjected her own thoughts and feelings into the conversations. I was impressed with this lady, with what she had to say, and with how much she wanted to help the people in the community. But, most of all, I was impressed with how easily and graciously she did it.

During the hours of conversation with the many families we visited, we always got around to asking them for their thoughts on how we could best help them to recover from the flood. The number one answer that people gave us centered on the desire for their children to have an education, and their fears about being unable to have the financial means to allow this to happen.

Even though most of the adults had little formal education themselves, they valued the importance of education. All of them wanted a better life for their children, one with a shot at decent jobs and a higher level of economic stability. These parents were living with the fear of not being able to provide for their children, and they didn't want their children to inherit that legacy.

At first, we didn't understand why there were so many financial burdens related to education. It was puzzling because we knew that the public schools in Mexico didn't charge tuition. We quickly learned about the hidden costs of education, which are often prohibitive for struggling families.

Although the Mexican schools don't charge tuition per se, they do have a number of fees that are required. They also have "voluntary" collections, that come with strong social pressures to participate. They become mandatory in the eyes of many parents. These fees and collections, along with school uniforms, books, supplies, shoes, and various other expenses can quickly add up to a financial burden that is beyond what many parents can provide.

Before leaving Villa Garcia, we sat down with Fran, Kiko, and Rosalia to review all that we had seen and heard during our visit. It was clear to all of us that education should be our focus. If we could do something to help the students to stay in school, then that would be the best thing that we could do for the parents and students. We talked openly about our hopes for students who would graduate. They would be in a better position to get jobs, become self-sufficient, and perhaps be able to help their own families. We envisioned these graduates as the next generation of community leaders, who would propagate the gift of education to their children.

When we arrived in Villa Garcia a few days earlier, we had no ideas on what might transpire. Now, we were beginning to develop a shared vision for how we might work together. Admittedly, the vision was somewhat cloudy, but this was a giant step from where we began. Now, the biggest question was how to proceed?

In three short days, Fran, Kiko, Rosalia, Abel, and Consuelo had become like a surrogate family, and being with them felt completely natural. Never had I connected so deeply and quickly with people who were complete strangers. Their acceptance and graciousness toward all of us made it apparent that they are guided by a commitment to live in harmony with other people, including those of different races and cultures. I basked in the warm glow of their presence, feeling safe and nurtured.

As we said our goodbyes, loaded the luggage and gifts into our cars, and prepared for the long trip home, my mind was on overload trying to process all of the events that had transpired over the last several days. It felt like a truckload of material had been dumped on the ground in front of me and needed sorting. But, at least I felt like we had the material to begin building a plan. That was a start.

On the drive back to Austin we were once again in three different cars, so there was not a chance for all of us to be together and talk things through. Maybe that was good. There were many hours on the drive home to get in touch with our individual thoughts and feelings and to discuss them with the others who shared our car. After arriving in Austin, we exchanged hugs and returned to our homes and families. In a few days the entire group would meet again to discuss everything. I couldn't wait to take the next step, even though I didn't know what it would be.

Our first gathering after the trip was electric. The travelers were joined by four others who were not able to make the trip. All of us were members of a class on social justice issues. The class, called JustFaith, is the single most important class that I have ever taken. The program has a motto which says that we change people and people change the world.

When our JustFaith group was first connected to Villa Garcia, there was a unanimous desire to learn more about the people in this village. We all wanted to do something to help them to recover from the devastating flood.

All of our class members had very busy lives, including jobs, families, young children, and a myriad of other commitments. What still amazes me to this day is that so many in our group were able to put everything on hold for a week, and travel to interior Mexico. That was no small undertaking. It included time off from work, arranging for child care for a week, and asking spouses in Austin to take on a lot of extra work during the trip.

The four class members who were not able to go truly wanted to do so, but for various practical reasons just couldn't. That didn't stop them from being fully invested in the project, helping with the planning, and supporting the travelers in every way that they could. Our team was solidly on board. We knew that our project would be focused on education for the students in Villa Garcia.

This team of people in Austin and Villa Garcia eventually became the nucleus for forming Weavers of Hope. Several others joined us including my wife, Martha, who has been our dedicated bookkeeper since the beginning. But the real heart and soul of Weavers of Hope is Fran, the person who is on the ground 24-7 in Mexico. Her dedication, commitment, love, vision, and determination are vital to all that we do. Without her, we would not exist. In 2008, Julieta became the first paid employee of Weavers of Hope. She brings creative ideas, energy, and passion to every part of our organization. Kiko and Rosalia continue to support our work in any way they can. Together, we are a very good team.

Each person on the trip, and each of those who did not get to travel to Villa Garcia, has played a vital role in our work with the people of Mexico. All of us are an integral part of the Weavers of Hope story. For my own part, I have been the president of Weavers of Hope from day one, a job that I have truly loved. My years in corporate America and the experiences since then have prepared me for this work. It has been a blessing for me to get to work on the things that I believe in, deep within my core. Getting out of bed each day is fun!

### 1st Trip to Villa Garcia
(February 2003)

The original JustFaith group from Austin connecting with our new friends
Front row: Rosalia, Beto, Ariana, Kiko. Back row: Carmen, Bonnie, Kay, Carol, Jack, Fran, Geri, Sandra, Olivia

Circa 2004: Rosalia, Beto, Ariana, Fany, Kiko
Family home – Kiko was born here with the help of a local mid-wife

Rosalia
Kiko's 'media naranja' – the other half of his orange

Consuelo, Maria, & Abel – 2010
Outside of the family home

Jack & Abel
At Abel's home

Fran – The heart and soul of Weavers of Hope
Pictured outside of her home in 2009

Fran
Early form of transportation – before getting an old pick-up truck

Don Chuy – local artisan
Carving mask from balsa wood

Villa Garcia
From a hilltop overlooking the village

Downtown Villa Garcia

Celebrating our first visit to Villa Garcia in back yard of one of the host families

Main street in Villa Garcia
Donkeys loaded with firewood for cooking. Many families don't have stoves or can't afford propane.

> *"So whoever is in Christ is a new creation: the old things have passed away; behold, new things have come."*
>
> The New American Bible (2 Corinthians, chapter 5, verse 17)

# Jack

As Kiko led us deeper into his native country, the endless desert landscape was hypnotic. My mind wandered off to philosophical questions of my own place in the world. What is the meaning of my life? Who exactly have I become? How did I get to this point? Do I like this person whom they call Jack? What am I going to do with the rest of my life?

In college I ran across a poster that said, "Today is the first day of the rest of your life." Beginning again with a clean slate seemed so hopeful. What a challenge it is to live a meaningful life and not default into an existence that is built around other people's ideas and expectations. Define who you want to be and live it. I daydreamed about the events that led up to this moment.

At this point in life, I was closer to being someone who I really liked than I had ever been before. I felt strongly connected to my one human family. I didn't want to see any of them suffering or living in abject poverty. I wanted everyone to be able to live with a sense of dignity. This level of caring and awareness had not always been present in my life.

At the same time, I was aware that even the best of my actions were full of mixed motives. There was a darker side of my being that was always looming in the background. There was a part of me that craved admiration, approval, respect, and recognition for my good deeds. Living with the tension between these two parts of my being was revealing and humbling.

Being the only child of two very loving parents made it easy for me to lean in the direction of being self-absorbed. In no way do I blame my parents for my own shortcomings. I take full responsibility for who I am. However, the environment that I grew up in made it a little easier to nurture my feelings of self-absorption.

I was not a difficult child for my parents to raise. I made mostly A's in elementary and middle school. Things came easy to me in the classroom, and I was able to focus my attention on the subject at hand. The combination of the two made school seem very simple. I followed the rules of my teachers, not wanting to make waves. All of this pleased my superiors, and made me look good in the eyes of my parents and teachers.

In eighth grade, I was selected to be the master of ceremonies for the school's major fund raising event, a program put on by the students. It was part of the May festival, a Saturday night program that attracted almost all of the parents and students. Stage fright introduced itself to me for the first time. On the eve of the big event my dad was trying to calm me down. He told me that everyone in the audience put their underwear on one leg at a time. I understood his theme, but was not overly relieved by the image. Most of all, I appreciated him listening to my concerns and trying to help me. It was one of the many ways that my parents told me that they loved me. They also frequently expressed their love in words.

At home, I typically followed the household rules regarding manners, chores, and other matters of daily living. My parents were loving, generous, and far from demanding. What they asked me to do seemed perfectly normal to me, and I was usually happy to do it.

One chore was different. I hated the job of pulling weeds out of the garden. I would get down on my hands and knees in the blistering sun of a New Orleans summer, and begin the ordeal. Enraging a mound of ants was the final insult. The way fire ants work is that they sneak up on you from all of the flanks, covering all of the exposed parts of the body. Then, the general of the battalion shouts, "Attack"! At that instant, every one of them bites. The pain shot me onto my feet and propelled me at lightning speed to the water hose to rinse them off. Fire ants are well named. Invariably, the damage was already done and the itching was without relief. By this time, I was cursing the ants, my parents, and the garden with the foul mouth of a sailor.

After five minutes of pulling weeds, I felt like I was scooping water out of the ocean with a thimble. The weeds were everywhere. They seemed to visibly multiply as soon as one of their brothers was ripped out of the earth. It felt like one could do this task for all of eternity without making a dent in their proliferation. And, I knew the ants were lurking, planning their next assault. Usually, my mom felt sorry for me after about an hour of this work and dismissed me. I felt like I had received a stay of execution from death row.

With all of the positive things going on in my life, it would seem like I would have been brimming with self-confidence. I wasn't. Like many adolescents, I focused on the things I didn't have, or in the case of pimples, the things I did have.

Pimples were a horror to me, especially the big red ones that lit up like neon signs on my face. I wanted to crawl into a hole and hide. The most embarrassing ones would cause me to try anything to disguise them. Skin toned pimple medicine to cover up their glare didn't work. When I inspected this cover-up, it usually looked worse than the glaring red. Sometimes I would try a little band aide, to provide cover. It made matters even worse. How could I claim that I cut myself shaving, when the number of my facial hairs could be counted on one hand? There was nothing to do but accept the degradation of it all. It was of little consolation to me that many of my friends were going through the same thing. My pimples seemed like the only ones in the world.

As a teenager, I had above average looks, athletic ability, size, strength, and intelligence. Yet, I focused on where others were ahead of me in all of these categories. This is not to say that I didn't breathe a tremendous sigh of relief that I was far from the bottom of my ranking system in these areas. Adolescence is a tough life passage for most kids. I was no different.

When I was a young boy, my dad's love of baseball mushroomed inside of me to a full passion for the game. We lived in the suburbs, a few miles outside of New Orleans, about a block from the levee which held back the Mississippi River. There was a big open lot next to our simple, little home. I would entertain myself for hours by tossing up rocks in the air and hitting them with my bat into the open pasture. Past the fence in the air was a single, past the tree a double, and over the tree a home run. Everything else was an out, a strike out occurring when I missed the rock completely.

Each player who came to bat was a member of the local professional team, the New Orleans Pelicans. They were a farm club of the Pittsburg Pirates in the National League. My dad took me to some of their games, and I became a huge fan of the team. When we went in person to see a game it was magical. I was enthralled by the size of the stadium and the professionalism of everything.

I followed all of their games on the radio and looked up the statistics in the local newspaper. I knew every player's batting average, pitching statistics, and lots of other little details. Once, my dad managed to get me an autographed ball by the players and team coach. It was a cherished prize.

In my simulated games with the rocks, I tried extra hard when my favorite players came up to bat. Some days I would play double headers (two games back to back). I just couldn't get enough of the thrill of baseball. With my faithful dog looking on it was all very innocent, like a scene in a Norman Rockwell painting.

Sports continued to be my driving interest until middle school. Then, things began to shift as I began to notice girls. At the boy-girl parties we danced, held hands, and sometimes played kissing games. That awakened feelings that surprised me. The normal bodily transitions were in full blossom.

After the parties, the parents would take us home. None of us had driver's licenses yet. I remember sitting in the back of a station wagon and holding hands with Diane, feeling like a superhuman stud. When everyone was finally dropped off, I told my best friend about my sexually stimulating experience. I felt a moment of panic when he told me that he had been holding her hand also. Little Diane was double dipping and creating wild fantasies in us. We both suffered a major dose of humiliation when we realized what she had pulled off.

From the time I was a little boy, my parents told me that I would be going to college one day. I never even considered any other option. It was what I was told was the next thing to do after completing high school. I went to a college preparatory high school with an excellent academic record. The foundation was being laid for my future, and I thank my parents for that, along with many other things. Neither one of them had finished high school. They had personally experienced the difficulties of earning a living with limited education. They wanted better for their son.

High school was a bit more challenging academically, especially chemistry and physics classes. Those little atoms and molecules just never made much sense to me. Nor did the concepts in physics. However, the other classes were much less challenging. My grades slipped a little, but were still mostly A's, so my parents were pretty happy with my performance. Sports, girls, and friends occupied every waking moment of my free time.

Basketball bumped baseball as my favorite sport. On weekends, we would often play pick-up games all day long. I never seemed to get tired on a basketball court. My abilities in the two sports allowed me to play on the high school junior varsity through my freshman and sophomore years. I was totally devastated when I got cut from the varsity teams in both sports. It felt like my world had ended.

As time passed, I realized that it was a lot of fun to be the bigger fish in the smaller pond. I joined every playground and recreation league that I could, never had to go to practice, and played only in the games. That eased the pain of not being on the varsity. It did not eliminate it.

I remember having three basketball games in one night, which also happened to be the night before our six-weeks exams in high school. My devious little mind was playing with how to get all of the games and the studying done. The perfect crime that I planned out was to fake being sick, stay home from school, study all day, then miraculously recover my health in time to head for the gym.

Of course my parents saw through this scheme and busted me. When my dad came home from work, we sat down to talk it all through. After they listened to everything, they decided to let me play the games that night. Included in the deal was that I would never skip school again. I really loved them for their merciful decision. I kept my part of the bargain and never skipped another high school class.

My college years were a time of learning, exploration, and partying, not necessarily in that order. I did what I needed to do to get mostly B's, and I worked at various jobs during the summers. Other than that, I drank, partied, and played sports.

Many of my friends from high school joined me at LSU in Baton Rouge, Louisiana, about 80 miles northwest of New Orleans. Baton Rouge is a vibrant port city on the Mississippi River, rich in culture, food, and music.

For us, it was like the city didn't exist. Life began and ended within a couple of miles radius of the LSU campus. My friends and I called LSU the country club. There was a student gymnasium, swimming pool, tennis courts, sports fields, golf course, and on and on. More importantly for me, there were unlimited parties, bars, diversions, and friends to hang out with.

The *creme de la creme* was the Saturday night home football games. LSU football games are a religious experience for almost everyone in Baton Rouge. Off-campus parties would start in the early afternoon. Since alcohol was not allowed on campus, this was a time of major indulgence. Then, there would be on-campus parties where we switched the emphasis from alcohol to food.

Finally, around 7 p.m. we'd begin the trek across campus heading for the football stadium, also known as Death Valley. In those days the stadium held

68,000 wildly enthusiastic fans. The residents of Baton Rouge loved their LSU Tigers as much as we students did. The crowd noises were deafening. Visiting teams could not hear their quarterback calling audibles or barking out the snap count. When they got penalized for a noise related infraction, the fans got even crazier and louder.

The football games were equally about winning and extending the party. When the game ended it was back to the parties with live music and more boisterous hooting and hollering. Football Saturdays were electric.

My classroom accomplishments were good, but far from excellent. Many opportunities for true growth were squandered, and I covered my insecurities with a know-it-all attitude and alcohol. I don't regret everything that happened, but I do regret many of the missed opportunities.

By graduation in 1968, I had shifted gears from hard partying to getting married and earning money. Materialism had set in, and I wanted to live the good life, one full of things. I got an offer to do computer work for Shell Oil Company in Houston. Since it was a good company in terms of salary and benefits, I decided to take the job. Within a week, I graduated, got married to my first wife, and moved to Houston. What an abrupt shift from the last five years at LSU!

I had been in Houston once before in high school with a group of my friends. It was the year when the 8th wonder of the world opened, the Astrodome, the first domed, indoor baseball stadium. Four of us piled into the car of one of our buddies and we spent the weekend drinking beer and watching the Houston Astros play. It seemed like a good omen that this would be my first home outside of Louisiana.

My hardest challenges at Shell came in the first two years there. I came into the job with no computer training from the university, and there was virtually no corporate training program. The theory was that I would learn from the older, more experienced people in the office and gradually come up to speed. The man who was my first mentor at Shell was a good programmer and a nice, easy-going guy. However, he left a lot to be desired as a teacher.

I had a good mind for piecing together information, sorting it out, and assembling a completed picture. However, in my first two years at Shell, I received only a few pieces of the information technology puzzle. I had no idea where the boundaries of the puzzle existed, and the parts were not color coded so that you could match up the yellow sections. I was totally and completely lost, positive that I would soon be fired for my complete lack of competence.

I had a friend at work who was also from Louisiana. We would confide in each other about how completely lost we were. He did get fired, and I knew that I would be next. Then, by the grace of God, I was assigned to another project with a new programmer as my leader. This guy was an outstanding teacher, and I was ravenously hungry for learning how to do this work. He saved my corporate life.

I had endless questions, and he had all the patience in the world to spend time with me and bring me along. I began to learn very quickly and to take in massive amounts of new information. The pieces to the puzzle were all out on the table, and I was matching them up quickly. What a tremendous relief that was for me! My career was on its way.

The other big challenge in the early years at Shell was in the collapse of my first marriage. I was devastated that my wife wanted to leave me. Whatever I had to offer was not what she wanted at that point in her life. To make matters more complicated, we had a baby son, Josh, whom we both dearly loved.

Together, we decided that it would be best for Josh to stay with me when we split up. She was hungry to live a single life, and I was ready to be a dad. Plus, I had the good job. Right from the start, I loved being a dad and having Josh with me. That felt right deep down within. It forced me to begin to mature.

Personally, as a young man who had been dumped, I felt shattered. My self-confidence dropped to very low levels, and I hurt more intensely than I ever had before. I tried to cover this over by acting macho and cool, like nothing bothered me. That was a complete charade.

I was probably the dumbest college graduate that ever existed. I didn't read any of the books or go to any of the support groups that help you deal with this type of a loss. I also didn't have much of a spiritual life to rely on. My family and friends were mostly in New Orleans. So, I had no one to talk with about what I was going through and how much I was hurting. In hindsight, I'm not sure I would have opened up to a close friend about what I was feeling. It seemed like a sign of weakness, and I desperately wanted to appear strong and unshakable.

Shortly after my separation, I began dating the woman who would become my current wife, Martha. She worked with me at Shell. We fell in love quickly and deeply. We have been married and best friends for 37 years. She is my *media naranja,* as Rosalia is for Kiko. Our daughter, Kennedy, was born in 1978. We were a family of four living, working, and growing up in Houston for many years.

Over the years, my spirituality began to slowly grow and mature. I started to find my own values and meaning in life. It took me many years to realize that

I was responsible for searching deep within myself for my core principles and acting on them. I could not simply adopt what my parents and others told me. It was my job to take complete responsibility for who I would become.

My mind wandered back to the end of my 25 years at Shell. It was a very good job, but it was not a job that I loved. I was so incredibly ready to leave the corporate world and experiment with previously untried work and activities. There was no longer a need for a salary, so that really opened things up. I tried a number of new things, including building decks with some friends, and doing income tax returns for 3 years with H&R Block and then for a small CPA firm.

However, my Spanish classes were the first true milestone events in my retirement. They opened doors to personal relationships with Latin American people, many from lower economic groups. Almost all of my life had been spent with people from my own race, culture, and economic level.

While in the middle of my Spanish language and cultural extravaganza, my mind was wonderfully receptive to new ideas and experiences. It was during this renaissance of learning that I began to look for opportunities to apply my Spanish on a more regular basis.

One of those openings came from *El Norte*, The North, a Spanish language newspaper in Austin. While looking through the pages, I stumbled across an ad that was seeking volunteers to teach English as a Second Language (ESL). I decided to give that a try. Many new opportunities seemed to keep emerging. My only problem was that I wanted to do them all.

Martha has always reminded me that I can shift into "race mode" on things which fascinate me, and sort of overwhelm myself, and those who love me most. Some restraint is a good thing, but it's not always easy to put on the brakes when life is popping.

For the first time in my life, I experienced significant diversity in my personal relationships. I was in direct contact with people from different cultures and economic groups. Some of them lived in poverty on the margins of our society. I got to spend time with them, hear their stories, and become their friend. Their trust in me softened a place in my heart. I began to experience compassion.

When I was a boy, my dad took me to see some of Tulane University's football games. Tulane was a small, private school with an excellent academic record. They were also a member of the Southeastern Conference, which meant that their sports teams had to compete against the mega schools, like Alabama, Florida, Georgia, and Louisiana State University, which would later be my alma mater. These contests were always a "David and Goliath" struggle for Tulane.

My Dad taught me to cheer for the underdog, hoping that a miracle would happen. Occasionally, it did. Somewhere in my heart, he instilled a desire to see the little guy win.

My Dad, a Jack also, was an intensely loyal man. After working for 45 years, he finally got to take his much anticipated retirement. He was still in good health, exercised daily, and began to play golf for the first time in his life. He loved to work on his golf game and visit with his buddies after they completed the 18th hole. Then, life tested him.

My Mom's health cratered and within a few years he became her full time caretaker. He gave up all of the things that he dreamed about doing in retirement. I marveled at his loyalty to my Mom as her conditions deteriorated and more was demanded of him each year. He never quit on her, giving more each year for 15 years until her death finally ended the pain. He is my example on loyalty.

My Dad was also a great listener, especially regarding the news of my life. He listened to me like few others ever have, and I felt about 10 feet tall to have him care so much about all of the aspects of my life. Showing me how to listen was one of my Dad's best gifts to me.

The Shell training group helped me to enhance this gift. They taught an excellent class on how to be an active listener. The secret was to listen for emotion or increased inflection in the voice of the speaker, then to ask follow-up questions in that area. The questions should be open ended and probe for the speaker's feelings about an issue. This technique sought more than a simple yes or no answer. Often, some much deeper feelings came out. Of course, all of this was related to managing employees in a productive and efficient manner.

However, these skills translated into all relationships. The combination of natural instincts and training helped me to be a good listener. I feel very good about that part of my personality. People tend to trust me, and truly appreciate how much I listen to their thoughts and ideas. Often they open up and go deeper into their feelings. Both of my children, Josh and Kennedy, are also very good listeners.

 As I drove into south Austin to teach ESL, it felt as though I had crossed the border into Mexico. Most of the signs were in Spanish. There was a predominance of Latin American people on the streets, and the sounds of Spanish music filled the air. I liked that south Austin provided me with an international flavor and the feel of being in another culture.

 Jose, my first ESL student, was the father of nine children. He had lived a life full of wonderful and varied experiences, one of which was being a "cowboy". His skills with horses allowed him to earn enough money for his family to survive. Jose was an older man whose education ended after first grade. He was a genuinely sincere, kind man with a simple joy for life. However, his ability to learn was limited.

 We spent some lovely time together and he truly enjoyed doing his homework. I enjoyed the chance to spend time with him and learn of his life and family. One of our classes was at the Mexican bakery that his son owned in this largely Hispanic part of town. He was proud to introduce me to his son, and pleased that he was now an official student in English class. I was honored to be his teacher and friend.

 It seemed like a rite of passage in later life for Jose to be involved in learning, just as his sons and daughters had done. I now live just a few blocks from that bakery, although the makeup of the neighborhood has changed significantly.

 While working with Jose, I was asked to add a class of advanced students. My job would be to let them practice conversation in English. It was easy to take this class on, as it was basically a free-flowing conversation in English. The topics we chose were things that were of interest to the group. Movies, politics, culture, sports, families, belief systems, weekend activities, dreams, fears, and a variety of other themes filled our class time with lively discussions.

 Latin American students made up the majority of the group, but I do remember one class that had 11 people from 8 different countries sitting around the table. On that particular day, we talked about how we honor the dead in our cultures. As this conversation unfolded we could look over at an elaborate Day of the Dead altar against the north wall of the meeting room. It was bright and festive, filled with flowers, candles, photos, food, and other memorabilia that were especially associated with deceased relatives and friends.

 In Mexico, and various other Latin American countries, this is a significant celebration to honor the dead. The food and drinks on the altar were some of the ones that the deceased people most enjoyed during their lives. It seemed like such a beautiful way of remembering and honoring our ancestors and friends.

Ever since that class, Martha and I have embraced this Latin American cultural celebration and made an altar in our home for our deceased parents and various other family members and special friends. It is very comforting to get out their photos, select the foods they enjoyed, and put out other things which remind us so clearly of them. My Dad gets a baseball and a golf ball on the altar. My Mom gets her favorite diet drink next to a Hershey chocolate kiss. She loved chocolate, and always had a bowl of Hershey kisses on her coffee table. People who visit our home often ask us about the altar, and some have even adopted the custom as a part of their own family traditions.

The people I met in the ESL classes got me out of myself and into the struggles that they faced in their daily lives. As an only child, I received an abundance of loving attention and care from my parents. I lived a safe life, free from daily struggles to survive. Being with the Latin American people helped me to become a little less self-centered. I am still working on that character flaw of mine. Ingrained habits change slowly.

The ESL classes were fascinating conversational and cultural experiences. As we got to know and trust each other, there was a bond that developed among us. Our discussions became more personal and revealing. When we talked about hopes, dreams, and fears, the level of the sharing sometimes caught me off guard. Everyone was so honest, respectful, non-judgmental, and accepting.

We learned from each other on many levels which went way beyond just learning English. For my part, I got to represent my country and my culture as I saw it, both good and bad. It was nice to be able to be so honest, and to have people listen so openly. In that group, we all seemed to have the innocent curiosity of children.

ESL and relationships with Latin American people have been an ongoing part of my life since that first class. The groups I've worked with have changed, but the personal connections have been consistently special. I love to be a part of the bonding process that happens with a new group as we begin to get to know and trust each other.

In our own small way we form a community and create an environment which allows the immigrants to relax. They get to have a time of acceptance and friendship, without some of the horrible discrimination that they frequently experience in their lives. My mind would sometimes flash back to the Tulane Green Wave football team and their epic struggles against all the odds. I thank my dad for sowing the seeds of caring for the underdog within me.

Occasionally, I was able to help my ESL students with some small aspect of their daily lives, and that was tremendously rewarding. Knowing that they felt secure enough to ask, told me that the trust levels between us were solid. They were in a new country, learning a new language, experiencing a new culture, and often without family. That was a tough life situation. I never asked about their legal status, but sometimes they told me. My goals were to be in caring relationships with them and to help them learn English. They helped me to appreciate all that I have. We have been good for each other.

Our ESL classes often evolved to the point where I could ask the students to tell me about ordinary things that they would like to learn – things that would make their daily living a little easier. The first time I asked this question, people talked of not being able to order from their favorite fast food menu. Martha and I went to the restaurant and asked for permission to take photos of the menu board. We spent the next couple of classes talking about the menu, learning the vocabulary, practicing ordering, adding up the bill, paying, and making sure we received the correct change.

Another routine problem that many of my students faced was that they didn't understand the "pay at the pump" options for buying gasoline for their cars. I had never really thought about all the questions which appear on the screen related to entering zip codes, selecting the proper fuel, receiving a receipt, and answering the other questions like those related to the car wash options.

Martha and I did a reconnaissance trip with our camera to the local station, took pictures of all the screens, and made paper copies that we could bring to class. It was exciting to see their faces light up as they learned what each screen meant. There are so many little things that aren't clear when your language abilities are minimal. Most of these things I took totally for granted until they asked me about them.

One late spring day, I was asking my group about what they were going to do during the summer when their kids were off from school. As we talked, I realized that most of them didn't know about all the wonderful services of the public library. As we talked, they got excited about the possibilities that the libraries offered.

We decided to devote the next few classes to the vocabulary and forms associated with obtaining a library card. I went to the local branch to get the forms and to understand exactly what was required. Together, we practiced everything, even role playing the actual event.

The culmination of these classes was that we met one day and car pooled to the library. The students used their newly acquired vocabulary to ask for a library card. They filled out the forms and received their official card. Then, they checked out their first installment of books and videos. Some of them even selected books on learning English. I was so very proud of them. More importantly, they felt extremely good about themselves and what they had accomplished.

One particularly touching story was with a group of students and three other instructors. We had divided the group into different levels based on the various ability levels in English. This particular group had been studying together for about three years, and considerable trust had developed among us. We sometimes extended our class time to celebrate birthdays and major holidays with food, desserts, and sodas.

Students brought their children to class with them and we usually provided child care. On the nights when child care was unavailable, it was not uncommon to be teaching at the white board with two or three little children bouncing off of my legs. I encouraged them to draw pictures on the bottom of the board, which they would proudly display at various times throughout the evening. Sometimes they were comic relief for us. Their innocence and purity were so sincere.

All of us were very comfortable with them as a part of the class. They were respectful of our lessons, and seldom demanded unreasonable attention. An occasional word or two of praise was all they needed before embarking on their next work of art. Sometimes when we were intently practicing vocabulary words, they would blurt out the English word with perfect pronunciation. When we all laughed, they were tickled. I always loved their presence during our class time, and their parents knew it and relaxed.

One evening we were talking and decided that it was time for some type of a field trip that would add a new flavor to our English classes. After a little investigating, we found a museum in central Austin that had an exhibit by Latin American artists. We arranged with the museum to provide a bilingual tour for our group and to reserve a room where we could celebrate after the tour with snacks and sodas.

Everyone came on this evening. Many of the students and teachers brought their family members and children. We were a diverse group. Many of the immigrant families had never been in downtown Austin. I tried to see this experience through their eyes. We were in an art museum in a major United States city, close to the state capitol building. The staff at the museum treated everyone with kindness and respect. The pride and sense of self-worth that I saw in the faces of our students was beautiful. I'll never forget that night. Tears well up in my eyes when I remember that story.

Luciano, my friend and former ESL student, was in that group. He left Mexico in the mid 1990s and illegally immigrated to the United States in order to find work so that he could care for his wife and children. There were no jobs for him in Mexico, and his family was desperate. When he arrived in the U.S. he started a yard care business, and sent most of his money back home for his family. He could not go back to visit since crossing the border without papers is often life-threatening. So, the years rolled by and he stayed here, worked, and sent his money home.

When we were studying the vocabulary related to the family, I would ask my students about their relatives, as a way of personalizing the lesson. I would ask, for example, what is your spouse's name, who are the parents of your spouse, and who are your children. One evening after class, Luciano came up and asked me if we could talk privately. He told me that his wife had left him and was living with another man in Mexico. He asked me to please not ask him any questions about his wife in class.

I could feel the pain I had caused him, albeit unintentional. What a devastating feeling that must have been for Luciano! Our conversation replays in my mind whenever I think of this gentle, kind man. He was so embarrassed by it all, and I could feel the shame in him. It touched me deeply, and in some small way, I could feel the hurt that he endured. I remembered my first wife choosing to leave me 25 years earlier. What incredible pressures on a man and woman when they are forced to live separately for so many years!

The connection between Luciano's story and the part of politics which relates to immigration policies, guest worker programs, keeping families together, and a whole range of human rights issues became very personal in my heart. I now see these issues not only through my eyes, but also through Luciano's. My connections to the Latin American people were growing in some powerful ways. I liked that I cared so much. I felt more human.

Around this time I met, Rebecca, an attorney who was running a non-profit organization which worked on the border in a *colonia,* which is basically a very poor neighborhood on the U. S. side of the border. The *colonias* are populated almost exclusively by Mexican people, some with legal papers and some undocumented. Rebecca's non-profit had formed a community group and she was helping the residents to obtain deeds to their property. Crooked land developers took their money but never provided them with deeds to the property that they had paid for.

Many years earlier, Rebecca made the decision to forego a large salary with a law firm in favor of working for much less money so that she could help those who are largely voiceless in our society. She dedicates her life to the quest for justice and fairness. She is one of my heroes.

Besides the help with obtaining clear titles to their land, the people in the *colonia* needed training on a whole range of financial things. They were totally unaware of how much interest is paid when someone makes only the minimum payment on a credit card each month. The other fees and tricks of credit cards were also largely an unknown for them. Similar problems existed with cell phones and their extra fees like roaming charges.

There were several other topics like these that would be helpful for the people to understand. Sometimes they needed loans, and the small loan companies often charged exorbitant interest rates. Rebecca suggested that we might want to do a training session on the interest payments that the small loan companies were charging. We also thought that it might be helpful to do a session on budgeting. I was excited to develop these classes, and go down to the border to present them in Spanish to various community groups. These conversations with the people of the *colonias* further solidified me with them, and drew me another step closer to their lives.

This work eventually led to Martha joining me to help the people in the office with computer related problems. Although Martha claims not to be a computer expert, she has many skills and talents in this area, along with being a gifted teacher. We were able to drive the six hours down to Rio Grande City together and work on these projects in their community. It was nice to have a travelling partner and confidant.

Rio Grande City, Texas is on the Texas-Mexico border between McAllen and Laredo. We lived in the *colonia* while we were visiting there. In the summer, which lasts a good six months there, the pounding heat is relentless. Added to that is the overwhelming dust. It forces you to cover your nose and mouth so as not to inhale it.

Temperatures frequently soared above 100 degrees Fahrenheit, and the sun beat down without mercy. There were few trees to provide pockets of refuge, and the heat slowly cooked us. The dust spread a layer of white film over the cactus plants which sprinkled the landscape. Just as the dust would begin to settle, another car would zoom by on the unpaved roads and stir up yet another cloud of swirling dust. The *colonias* are usually without paved roads, and sometimes without running water. Often, city services are dreadfully lacking or non-existent.

Through all of these experiences in ESL and working on the border, my life slowly became more intertwined with the people of Latin America and the struggles they face. I have gradually fallen in love with these people. Their kindness and simplicity, their perseverance and determination, and their genuine thankfulness for the smallest little things that are done for them is heart wrenching.

These connections with Latin American people were slowly forming me for the work of Weavers of Hope. However, at that time I had no idea that this was where my life was headed.

This cultural awakening has been a path which I never would have expected to be walking on, but I'm there, and I think that this is where God wants me to be at this point in my life. I was joking around with one friend that if I believed in reincarnation, I would probably return as a Mexican. She laughed and said, "Jack, how many Mexicans do you know with bald heads and fair skin?" So, maybe I'd have dark skin and a full head of thick black hair. That thought puts a smile on my face.

I guess the seeds of change had been germinating for many years, but more started to sprout during the two years of my formal Spanish classes. In the summer of 2001, Martha and I were invited to join a group that would be studying and experiencing various issues related to social justice using a curriculum that was developed by JustFaith Ministries in Louisville, Kentucky. The program was described as an intensive, eight month, educational and experiential study of social justice. The program linked the message of the gospels to a life of compassion and becoming involved with people who live on the margins of society. That terrified me. I didn't want to move any farther out of my comfort zone. Yet, I was inwardly fascinated by this way of thinking and living.

My defense mechanisms were surging and creating a slew of reasons why I couldn't possibly make this type of commitment. After all, eight months is quite a lot to ask! When the person making the offer, calmly and gently said that she guessed this wasn't the right time in our life, I almost wanted to scream…*Yes, I do want to do it, convince me.* She simply invited us to think about the invitation and get back to her later with our answer. There was no pressure or timetable from her, only an offer.

Martha and I decided that if we were going to take this class, then we should take it together. We realized that it had the potential to bring about serious change in us and in our lives, and we wanted to go through the experience as a couple. We have always worked at having a good marriage, and staying close. Within 24 hours, it was clear that we wanted to give this a try. I would have to move into the unknown and deal with my fear. We signed up the next day.

As I walked into the classroom on that first day, it seemed rather cold and stark. The neon overhead lights and the white paint on the walls didn't contribute to a warm, cozy feeling. However, the surroundings became immediately irrelevant. The content of the class completely overshadowed everything else, right from the start. The subjects we explored and discussed, along with the readings and videos, added the richness, color, and zest to what the meeting room was lacking.

On the first day, as we took our break, I walked past a reception room that was showing footage of two planes crashing into the twin towers at the world trade center. It was almost surreal, as the horrors of the tragedy became evident. I will never forget the day of my first JustFaith class, 9/11/2001. I wondered if that was an omen.

During the curriculum, issues like poverty, exploitation, and injustice leapt off the pages at me as I read books and Biblical texts which became alive and challenging. Teachings like those in the Sermon on the Mount moved me in amazing new ways. How could I have dismissed these readings for so many years? How could I not hold myself accountable to these core teachings? I don't know the answers to those questions, but I do know that JustFaith caused deep stirrings within me. Something clicked in my head and in my heart, and I was open to change, dramatic change.

The eight months were like a birthing process which resulted in a new me, one that felt a longing to make a deeper connection with the people of all races and cultures who share this earth with me – my one human family. I could feel the inherent dignity of each person, and could never again choose to ignore them. I was driven to make changes in my life so that I could do a better job of living in solidarity with other people. For the first time, the poor and powerless moved to the top of my list.

During this time of education and opening, there were several opportunities for direct contact with people who lived on the fringes of society. One that really impacted me was a work project with three men who used to be homeless. They had gotten off of the streets and were living in a sort of half-way house, trying to transition into new lives. The two people who lived in and monitored the house had a strong personal investment in helping their guests. On our project together, we cleaned up the yard, hauled the trash to the dump, and then went out for lunch. As we ate our burgers and talked, I got to really see these guys as people who were more like me than I wanted to admit. It was a thought provoking connection, and would soon be followed by other similar experiences.

Things were happening fast inside of me, and it felt right. More right than anything had in a long time. I was receiving an education that was different from what I had learned in the university, and my heart was beginning to really feel compassion. I learned to cry. It was a time of great awakening for me.

*"We plant the seeds that one day will grow.*
*We water seeds already planted, knowing that they hold future promise.*
*We lay foundations that will need further development.*
*We provide yeast that produces effects far beyond our capabilities."*

Oscar Romero

# Beginning Weavers of Hope

Before a field is ready for planting, farmers do a considerable amount of preparation. Getting rid of the rocks and weeds, tilling the soil, and installing the irrigation system are some of the preparation work that results in a bountiful harvest. It was the same thing with getting ready to form Weavers of Hope, only I had no idea of what I was preparing for. The events that were to come were completely unknown, but there was a vague sense that something might be on the horizon.

There were two formative events that occurred before that first trip to Villa Garcia, before we would ever meet Fran, Kiko, Rosalia, Abel, Consuelo, and Maria. In fact, these events happened before I knew that there was such a place as Villa Garcia. In hindsight, it seems like they unfolded at just the right time to prepare us for the work that would come.

The first event happened in El Salvador. The second was in a JustFaith class, which focused on domestic and international poverty. Let me begin in El Salvador.

Tensions had been escalating during the 1970s between the military-led government of El Salvador and the Farabundo Marti National Liberation Front (FMLN), a coalition of five left-wing militias. The FMLN was challenging the alliance of the right-wing military and the tiny group of wealthy land owners. This alliance spurned fraudulent presidential elections in 1972 and 1977. The coalition organized huge demonstrations and demanded fair elections and improved social conditions. The government fought back violently to maintain power.

Most Salvadorans were *campesinos,* farmers, living in poverty without running water or electricity. A tiny privileged minority lived in wealth and opulence. The regime's token land reform did little to alleviate the economic inequity. The government responded to the political unrest with state-of-siege declarations, the suspension of constitutional rights, and paramilitary death squads. These death squads were responsible for brutal torture and widespread killings as they rooted out their opponents.

U. S. ambassador Robert E. White assessed the situation as follows:

*"The major, immediate threat to the existence of this government is the right-wing violence. In the city of San Salvador, the hired thugs of the extreme-right, some of them well-trained Cuban and Nicaraguan terrorists, kill moderate-left leaders and blow up government buildings. In the countryside, elements of the security forces torture and kill the campesinos, shoot up their houses and burn their crops. At least 200 refugees, from the countryside, arrive daily in the capital city. This campaign of terror is radicalizing the rural areas, just as surely as Somoza's National Guard did in Nicaragua. Unfortunately, the command structure of the army and the security forces either tolerate or encourage this activity. These senior officials believe, or pretend to believe, that they are eliminating the guerillas."*

The civil war in the tiny country of El Salvador (1980-1992) killed over 75,000 people. During this same period in history, similar things were happening in other Central American countries, including Guatemala, Honduras, and Nicaragua.

During the Carter, Reagan, and Bush administrations, the United States sent seven billion dollars of foreign and military aid to El Salvador in ten years. Many thought that the money was used by the Salvadoran government to fund massive killings among the campesinos. The existence of these death squads was a controversial issue in the U.S. in the mid 1980s. Critics of this aid alleged that the U.S. feared the spread of communistic regimes close to our homeland, and indirectly supported the death squads. After a six-month investigation, the United States Senate Select Committee reported that there was no evidence to support this allegation.

◆ ◆ ◆

In May of 2002, I decided to take a mission awareness trip to El Salvador with the Christian Foundation for Children and Aging (CFCA), a non-profit organization which provides educational sponsorships for young people and help for the elderly. The organization was actively working in 26 countries with sponsorships exceeding 250,000 at that time.

They believe in the potential of the poor to effect change in their own lives and in the world. This is done primarily through education. They connect individual sponsors with a child, youth, or elderly person in need of encouragement and support. Families living in poverty are struggling heroically to overcome tremendous odds. CFCA members affirm their dignity by becoming their friends and walking with them on their journey.

Martha and I had been sponsoring Marta, a teenage girl in El Salvador, and exchanging letters with her for a couple of years. The desire to make more of a personal connection with Marta was one of the things that prompted me to sign up to visit her in El Salvador. I wanted to learn more about her life and how she and her family lived.

The foundation encourages sponsors to visit their sponsored students by taking part in a mission awareness trip. These trips give you an opportunity to experience firsthand how your sponsorship helps young people to overcome the obstacles of poverty. You see how education, nutrition, clothing, and medical care offer hope for families in desperate need. You also get to see how your sponsorship empowers people to reach out in compassion to others in their community.

When you visit the local projects that the foundation sponsors, you travel not as a tourist but as an honored guest and friend of the local people. You experience the hospitality of the poor, who generously share all that they have with you. You learn about their social and economic realities, and are often inspired by their spirituality.

This sounded like exactly the experience I was looking for.

The five of us, all CFCA sponsors, travelled to El Salvador from various cities in the United States. We were met at the airport in San Salvador, the capitol city, by two foundation representatives.

El Salvador is bordered by Guatemala and Honduras to the north and the Pacific Ocean to the south. As we drove the 40 miles to the northwest from the airport, I remember watching the rich tropical landscape ascend into picturesque, lush mountain ranges. Sadly, I also noticed that a significant amount of trash was scattered along the highway, desecrating the otherwise verdant countryside. Our destination was Santa Ana, a small city which would be our headquarters for the next week.

Upon arriving in Santa Ana, we drove beyond the gate of a modest brick home and parked next to the house. I saw barbed wire and jagged glass lining the top of a seven foot fence of concrete blocks. We were not allowed to leave the compound without being accompanied by CFCA staff. It jolted my mental visions of hikes in the surrounding mountains during our free time. The two guest bedrooms where we stayed were divided by gender. Each had three sets of bunk beds in them. Space would not be a problem for me as there was only one other man in our group of five.

The home also included a sleeping area for staff and some modest office space for their work projects. Most of the staff returned to their homes and families in the evenings, but there were always at least two of them who stayed in the compound with us. Our safety was obviously at the top of their priority list.

The five of us who were on this trip were taken around to various foundation projects in the area, which consisted primarily of schools and orphanages. We had the opportunity to talk with teachers, students, and parents, and to be invited into some of their homes. Typically, the homes had dirt floors, leaky roofs, and no running water or electricity. The poverty of their living conditions was brutally obvious.

There was also a day set aside for all of us to spend with our sponsored students and their families. On that day we journeyed south to the coast and met in a beautiful little park with picnic areas and swimming. It seemed so radically different from the harsh living conditions of the families. I imagined what a special day this probably was for them, one that provided a brief respite from their daily struggles.

I had the opportunity to meet the student who Martha and I had been sponsoring for several years, along with her family. Marta was a shy 14-year-old girl with a gentle smile and a sense of innocence. Her parents were very outgoing, friendly, and talkative. They brought me a bag of sweet, juicy mangos which were grown on their land. The juice ran down my forearms as I cut away the peeling and bit into my first of several mangos.

The CFCA staff members were an impressive group of young, motivated, caring adults, who were dedicating their lives to helping the people in El Salvador, a poverty ravished country. Many of them had lived through the horrors of the ruthless civil war which had ended only ten years earlier. The atrocities and events of the war were still fresh and raw in their minds. Some of them had survived the torture and death of their loved ones. They remembered soldiers invading their universities, clandestine study groups meeting in homes, and the fear of daily living. There was an eerie horror in their eyes as they told the stories.

Somehow, out of this devastation, the CFCA staff members were able to persevere and unite in hopes of a better future. Their resilience and ability to continue on amazed me. Much of the foundation's help is focused around the central belief that education can help to lift people out of poverty. Educated citizens then take an active role in shaping the future of their country. That concept made sense to me. I sure didn't have a better answer for how to do it. Less than a year later, this same concept would become the foundation for the work of Weavers of Hope in Villa Garcia.

Amidst this tragic history and widespread poverty, there was often a happiness and joy that existed in the faces of the people we met. Family bonds and spirituality were noticeably strong, perhaps even more so than in my own life.

Along the road going to the CFCA projects, I'd see families sitting together outside their tiny homes. They would be talking, watching the kids play soccer, or just puttering around. Often there was music and laughter surrounding these families. Their little communities seemed to provide safe harbors for healing the emotional wounds of the war. Time seemed to be abundant for them in their simple, rural environment. On this trip I learned that you could live through war, tragedy, and poverty and still maintain dignity and hope. There was also a pervading sense of acceptance which went beyond my comprehension.

I was beginning to see a common thread running through the events of my more recent life. The passion for learning Spanish, the desire to spend time with Latin American people, the concern for those who are struggling, and the connection with the Salvadoran people seemed to be linked.

On the flight back to the United States I sat next to the founder of CFCA, Bob Hentzen. The time whizzed by for me as he told stories of his relationships with the people of El Salvador and various other countries. He had been to all 26 of the countries where they provided sponsorships.

We talked of his work and beliefs. I pondered what he had accomplished since beginning his work from ground zero in 1980. It seemed hard to believe that over a quarter of a million people were being given hope, all because of his vision and leadership.

My time with Bob was another step for me into a life of solidarity with those who live very differently than I do. I felt a premonition that my life was going to be shaped in some way by these events, but how it would play out was unclear. Weavers of Hope would soon provide the clarity.

The second formative event that occurred before being introduced to the people of Villa Garcia was the JustFaith class. It would provide education, motivation, and a desire to make a difference in the world.

The original JustFaith program was introduced by Jack Jezreel in a parish in Louisville, Kentucky. It was immediately and dramatically successful. Since then, churches around the country have had similar results. The JustFaith programs transform people and expand their commitment to the work of social justice. Over 18,000 people from 1,000 faith communities across the country have participated in JustFaith programs. Rooted in the words of Scripture, people are encouraged to care for the poor and vulnerable. For many, it is a journey outside of their comfort zones into the lives of those who live without the basic necessities of life.

Ten years later, I am still involved in the JustFaith movement, for these same reasons. The ripple effect of people who work together for peace and justice is powerful. Being with people who were committed to this way of living was extremely attractive. They inspired me and lifted me up. I did not want to disappoint them.

There is an often used analogy that says that if you give a person a fish, they have food for a day. But, if you teach a person to fish they have food for a lifetime. JustFaith takes it a step farther and says that sometimes you have to rip down the fence around the pond so that everyone can dip their line into the water. The ripping down of the fences is equally important. Usually, this is a much tougher job.

A direct handout is relatively easy to do if your heart is moved toward treating someone with charity. Teaching and preparing a person to do it on their own is more time consuming and difficult, but still can be accomplished in most cases with the investment of time. But the fences come down very slowly and only after considerable work. William Wilberforce, the British politician and philanthropist, headed the parliamentary campaign against the British slave trade for 26 years until the passage of the Slave Trade Act of 1807. He, like many others, was ripping down fences. He had to be both persistent and patient.

We learned in class about the importance of all aspects of caring. Solidarity begins with building relationships. From that can come immediate help, training for self-sufficiency, and the ripping down of fences. I felt myself being drawn into the philosophy of the longer term solutions, but had no idea where or how to begin this type of work. It was all new and often overwhelming. But, the pull was there. There was also a fear of the unknown and where this would all lead.

In El Salvador, we learned about Archbishop Oscar Romero, the death squad's most infamous assassination. He was a man who was ripping down fences. Earlier in his life he was strongly connected to the wealthy, elite landowners and "the church of the rich". His personal seeds of change began to sprout, and his solidarity with ordinary Salvadoran people grew. His life was never the same after that.

Over time, he began to speak out against the exploitation by the rich of the masses who lived in stark poverty. He became the voice of the people, and they flocked to him as their spokesman in their hope for a better life. Those in power were furious that Romero challenged the status quo. It cost him his life. He was assassinated in church in 1980, the latest in a string of killings of those who advocated change.

Standing up for the poor was fine until it challenged the power structures of the rich. Then, it was very dangerous, even life threatening. The cycles of concentrated wealth, injustice, exploitation, and revolution seem to repeat themselves throughout history. Sadly enough, the new power groups are often as oppressive as those they replace. Romero's words have remained with me:

*"We plant the seeds that one day will grow.*
*We water seeds already planted, knowing that they hold future promise.*
*We lay foundations that will need further development.*
*We provide yeast that produces effects far beyond our capabilities.*
*We cannot do everything, and there is a sense of liberation in realizing that. This enables us to do something, and to do it very well.*
*It may be incomplete, but it is a beginning, a step along the way, an opportunity for the Lord's grace to enter and do the rest."*

Some of the seeds which Romero sowed during his lifetime would begin to sprout in the spring of 2010. For the first time since the devastating civil war, the FMLN party would win the country's presidential election.

Mauricio Funes, a former television journalist, would become president of El Salvador, declaring it the happiest day of his life. He pledged to respect all

Salvadorian democratic institutions, and to begin a new chapter of peace for his country. He strongly rejected the idea that he would be a puppet of Venezuala's President Hugo Chavez, and committed himself to maintaining good relations with the United States.

At the same time, he acknowledged the magnitude of the problems that were awaiting him. El Salvador had one of the world's highest murder rates. Coupled with that sobering fact was the severity of the world's economic downturn. The task which awaited him was daunting.

The trip to El Salvador in the summer of 2002 was my first trip with the sole focus being on social awareness and the intention of following the experience with action. The events of my life and my connection with the Latin American people had been evolving steadily and naturally for some time with one thing leading easily into the next. The little things that were developing in my head and heart were often not particularly noticeable in the daily flow of life.

As I reflected on the events of the last several years, the path seemed clearer and more deliberate. Looking at the world and learning more about the realities that existed was the beginning. That led into forming relationships with people who were struggling to survive. From that came compassion and a desire to do something.

Looking at things in this way allowed me to detach just a little from my life of comfort and ease. It created a desire to become engaged in social issues. It also created an unanticipated sense of wonder and excitement as each new day began. My life had a focus and a sense of purpose.

The next year of JustFaith classes began a couple of months after I returned from El Salvador. I was returning to JustFaith for the second year as a co-facilitator. My experiences from the first year were so enriching, that I wanted to be a part of helping the next group that would go through the program.

The new group had its own dynamics, quite different from the prior year. The meetings continued to be stimulating. I felt more grounded as I read the books and watched the videos for a second time. I had wondered if the material would lose a little of its impact and zest on the second time through. That was not the case. Rather, it was like watching a favorite movie for a second time, and picking up on many of the little details that were missed in the first viewing. The discussions were new and fresh, and the insights and reactions of the others in the group continued to fascinate me, as they had a year earlier.

I liked being a part of this little community with people who were interesting, enriching, frustrating, and surprising. Within me, the deeper yearnings for a stronger connection with other people and cultures continued to grow. My experiences in El Salvador added a backdrop for a deeper exploration of international issues. Many of the same thoughts and insights from the prior year became clearer, and more locked into my psyche. I was glad to still be riding this wave of learning, energy, and social awareness.

Not long after the second JustFaith class had begun, in the fall of 2002, our group got some unexpected news. Carol, our lead facilitator, came to class one day with a new story to tell. This was not unlike Carol, as she was always open to new ideas, developing situations and opportunities to be active in the work of social justice and helping others.

Barely over five feet tall, she was a force – small in stature, but gigantic in heart and energy. She celebrated her sixtieth birthday that year, but it was hard to think of her in terms of age. People tended to think of her as a powerful presence - caring, dynamic, vibrant, and full of passion.

In lieu of presents for her birthday gathering, she asked that we chip in to buy a farm animal through Heifer International. It is an organization which helps small farmers to obtain a sustainable source of food and income. We were glad to do that. It seemed to be the appropriate gift for Carol, one that allowed her to receive and give at the same time.

Carol always had strong opinions which she freely shared. She also listened to others with interest and openness. Her work on justice and peace projects, both domestic and international, was exemplary. But, other little stories about her life trickled out during these two years of JustFaith classes. I began to wonder "where she ended". She would casually drop a line like "while I was fixing my roof" or "I had to attend a fireman's training class" or "I love to do my clown act". I found myself smiling when one of these lines popped out and wondering how many more things she did that I'd never know about.

On this particular morning, Carol relayed to us a conversation that she had with her friend, Fran, who had been living in Villa Garcia, Zacatecas, Mexico since 1998. This was the first time we learned that such a place existed.

Fran had told Carol the tragic story of a flood which surprised everyone in the village, and caught them totally unprepared. Two people were killed, and several others injured. Many of the simple little homes in Villa Garcia had been either destroyed or badly damaged in the catastrophe. Home furnishings were piled in the streets with the putrid smell that comes after an event like this.

Years later, shortly after hurricane Katrina, I would visit my cousin in Slidell, Louisiana, about 60 miles northeast of New Orleans. They got the full brunt of the hurricane, as did several small towns on the Mississippi gulf coast. As we began to clear out the destruction at my cousin's home, I experienced the smells of rotting food and water soaked mattresses. They were nauseating. Like the post Katrina times, the streets of Villa Garcia were lined with the ruined possessions of a lifetime. Mud was everywhere, as hillsides slid into town and mixed with the flood waters.

The cause of the Villa Garcia tragedy was an earthen damn that unexpectedly caved in during the early morning hours. The rupture released the waters of a mountain reservoir which sat above town and supplied water to the village. The small canal which ran through the center of Villa Garcia could not hold the deluge, and the raging waters quickly overflowed the banks and wreaked their havoc. The previously life-giving water for the village was now a life taker and a property destroyer. What had been a sleepy little pueblo was now a scene of devastation. Fran told Carol of the people's desperation.

Prior to the flood, the village was a typical, poor, rural Mexican pueblo. Now, the people were stunned, as if having taken a shot to the head, and not sure what to do next. Meager little savings were quickly depleted in the rebuilding process. Homes without structural damage still needed mattresses, refrigerators, and all of the things which fill a home. Fran, like the rest of the villagers, wasn't quite sure what to do next, but she needed to tell someone the story, and that someone was Carol.

As Carol relayed all of this to us, she also shared a few pictures that had come via the internet. They vividly portrayed the situation. We were truly sorry that this happened to Fran and her community members, but none of us in the JustFaith class knew what we could do. However, all of us wanted to learn more about the situation. We wanted to look for opportunities to help the people of Villa Garcia as they recovered from the devastation.

I volunteered to contact Fran via e-mail. In my first e-mail I wrote that we wanted to help, but that we had no idea what we could do from Austin, some 800 miles north. That e-mail note would be the beginning of a deep friendship between Fran and me, and would eventually lead to the formation of a nonprofit organization called Weavers of Hope.

Over the next few weeks, Fran and I exchanged several e-mails. She did not have a phone in her home, and long distance calls on public phones were expensive. I would bring weekly updates to our JustFaith class members and we would spend a little time during our meetings talking about the situation and the plight of the people of Villa Garcia.

Out of those conversations came the idea that we should send a delegation from our class to the village to meet the local people and assess things more thoroughly. It seemed like this tragedy was directly linked to the type of social situations that JustFaith was training us to deal with. Maybe this was the time for us to move from the theoretical into the actual. Perhaps our class project had come as unexpectedly as the waters from the dam that blew out in the hills above Villa Garcia.

We began to prepare for the trip. Safety concerns surfaced, along with other challenges like finding the village, driving time, accommodations in the village, translation, what we wanted to accomplish, and who we should talk with. None of these things were major impediments for us. The group was committed to working through the obstacles and finding a way to become involved. Eventually, we agreed that February 2003 would be the time to go, approximately six months after the flood.

These were the formative events that happened less than a year before that first trip to Villa Garcia.

After that first trip to Villa Garcia, our next JustFaith meeting was bubbling with excitement. Those who were not on the trip were anxiously awaiting the report out. They had been mentally and spiritually with us for the last week. Those of us who had been in Villa Garcia, and now had several days to let it all settle, were ready to talk.

The stories began to pour out, along with ideas, emotions and feelings. After a wonderfully rich conversation, we unanimously agreed that we wanted to follow the advice of the people of Villa Garcia and provide educational sponsorships for their children. It seemed like a great place to begin.

Carol was scheduled to do a presentation to several hundred people as part of a spiritual mission in a few weeks. She would use her time to speak of Villa Garcia. She would tell the story of the flood, the trip, the conversations with the parents and their desire to educate their children. Then, she would ask people to sponsor a student for $20 per month to help with their education related expenses.

She felt sure that many people would respond. I hoped that she was right, and as it turns out, she was. Forty people signed up to sponsor a student – a great first response. Carol's dynamic personality and credibility in the community were the most important things that allowed this project to get off to such a successful start. We were off and running.

Meanwhile, back in Mexico, Fran, Kiko, and Rosalia were selecting the best student candidates from Villa Garcia to receive this financial support. Students were chosen based on a variety of qualities, including academic ability, supportive parents, attitude, ethics, community service, and need. It was generally felt that younger students would get one sponsor, and older students two or three, because their education costs were higher.

The selected students ranged from elementary school age through those who were in the university. The reason for bringing university students into the program was that they were closer to being able to graduate and make a positive impact on their families and the community. We would later learn that there were many other reasons that made this an excellent strategy.

I thought about my experiences in El Salvador with CFCA, and realized that we were planning to do exactly what they had been doing quite well for the last 23 years. I was confident that I could contact their founder, Bob Hentzen, and that he would adopt Villa Garcia into the CFCA family of projects. As luck had it, I had shared the plane ride from Guatemala to Houston with him only a few months earlier. We knew each other. Thankfully, it would not be a cold call. Plus, Martha and I were already on their list of sponsors. That should be another small factor which would give us credibility.

Through my naïve eyes, it seemed like we wanted to give CFCA a beautiful gift. We had found a village with a strong leader, Fran. She was supported by two strong community leaders with local savvy, education, wisdom, and integrity, Kiko and Rosalia. We would present them with 40 sponsors, 20 hand-picked students, and everything already in place and ready to go.

CFCA would not be burdened with needing to find a local project manager, recruit new donors, or find deserving students. We would package all of this up as a gift and hand it to them – a turnkey operation. It seemed like a perfect fit, a match made in heaven.

I thought that they would be ecstatic to expand their circle of support to the students in Villa Garcia. Since they had other sites in Mexico, they would not have to add the overhead of getting established in a new country. I was smugly smiling on the inside at how neatly all of this was fitting together.

It was time to call Bob and share with him the details of the wonderful gift that we had for CFCA. I was brimming with excitement and confidence. Quickly, but gently, he popped my bubble. The story he told me was that every week or two he received a similar offer from one of the 26 countries where they were working. He said that it was impossible for them to accept these offers. It was too much, too fast. They would need to check out everything to insure that it fit into their overall mission and met all of their requirements. Often, they had their own waiting list of sites and projects, without needing other people to provide ideas for where they might go next.

However, he expressed great belief in what we were trying to do. He talked of other people who had hopes similar to ours. Some of them had gone forward on their own. He encouraged us to do the same. He suggested that we work with his staff and learn the details of how they do things. Basically, he said that we could model ourselves after their organization and learn from them.

I was really disappointed with the outcome of this conversation. I had convinced myself that CFCA would readily accept the Villa Garcia project. I envisioned that there would be a fairly large investment of initial work to get everything in order for them to take over. But, I thought that it would be a onetime expenditure of effort. I foresaw them taking over full operation after the turnover. The most ongoing work that I could envision was to perhaps do occasional presentations to raise awareness for the work that they do. I hated to see us have to take on all of the work that would be involved in running a sponsorship program. That seemed like a large step to take. None of this was going as I had planned.

I brought the disappointing news to our group. Together, we accepted the setback. After some conversation and discernment, we decided that we should press on ourselves, just as Bob Hentzen had suggested. The group asked me to follow up on the offer to speak with the CFCA staff and begin studying how they operate.

I was proud of our collective will to keep going. We were a band of volunteers with no experience at doing this type of a project. We would be operating between two countries and cultures, without any paid employees. Yet, none of us could let go of our desire to help the people of Villa Garcia. The connections with them were made, and we remembered their faces and stories. Their desperation and desire for better lives for their children was a fresh, vivid memory. So, we went forward.

I had several hours of telephone conversations with the people in CFCA's headquarters in Kansas City. They were gracious to a person, willing to share all that they do and how they do it, and encouraging. I took copious notes, and thanked each one of them.

Now, eight years later, I have many of the same feelings that I think the CFCA staff probably had at that time. It doesn't really matter whether a student is supported through CFCA, Weavers of Hope, or any of the other similar sponsorship programs that exist. What matters is that people are in relationship with one another, people from all economic groups, countries, races, and cultures. The concept that all of us on planet earth are one human family has become one of my core beliefs.

This was the solidarity that we had learned about in JustFaith. It gave us a vision of a more just society, one where everyone can live in dignity and with the basic necessities of life. That definition of unity has now taken root inside of me. It has moved from a learned concept to a principle that I want to guide my life. I feel sure that this shared vision is what motivated the CFCA staff to open up their organization and their hearts to us. CFCA was and still is a very classy organization. We work hard to make Weavers of Hope the same.

Initially, Carol took the lead on the Austin end, collecting sponsorship money, handling sponsor questions, keeping the books, mailing the money to Mexico, etc. Fran was our leader in Mexico, and was deeply involved with our first group of sponsored students and their families.

The rest of us volunteered to do bits and pieces of the work, but the truth is that it was fragmented. We used a variety of techniques depending on the individual volunteers who were helping. The work was being done on everything from simple computer spreadsheets to notes written on the back of a page. We were limping along, but we had started. Sponsorship money was flowing in and getting through to the families in Villa Garcia who desperately needed it. All of us felt very good about that accomplishment.

Inwardly, while experiencing the joy of being able to help the people of Villa Garcia, I worried about the loose formation that we were flying in. All of my corporate life had been centered on business plans, timetables, organization, accountability, audits, and smoothly functioning business entities. When I realized how far we were from this it made it hard for me to sleep at night.

Part of me wanted to ignore these issues and figure that it would all work out fine. Another part of me wanted to take it on, organize it, model it more closely to CFCA, and get it into a well-managed project format. This latter desire was tempered by knowing how much work that it would be. I was not at all sure if I was willing to commit that much time and energy. I actually sat with that dilemma for several months, talking things over with Martha, and letting it all settle. She helped me with the analysis and the unique insights that she always has to offer.

During those months we got a closer look at many of the things that were related to running a successful organization. As Fran expressed her tremendous appreciation for the work that we were doing in Austin, she also spoke of long waiting lists of students who hoped for entry into our program. The needs in the village were great. New students would require us to find more funding.

It became obvious that we needed to develop a system for recruiting new sponsors. We needed a system for translating letters and allowing them to flow smoothly between students and sponsors. When sponsors missed payments, it became clear that we needed some type of a reminder system. As the calendar year wound down, it was time to send out receipts to our sponsors and donors so that they could use their donations on their tax returns as charitable contributions. This was a huge issue that we had not really thought much about.

The work was growing exponentially. We were beginning to get a better practical understanding of what was involved. Attracting additional sponsors and students would add time to all of our work tasks. We were beginning to appreciate how much supporting work goes into making a successful organization like CFCA. Top notch organizations don't happen by accident.

Fran was fully immersed in the work in Villa Garcia. She was working with the students and their families, checking up on grades, providing counseling, and funneling out sponsorship money to the selected students. Fran originally went to Mexico in 1998 because she felt like that was where God was calling her to be. She went without a plan and without knowing what she would be doing. She went only with the belief and trust that it would all work out. As our educational sponsorship program evolved, Fran began to see her calling in Mexico take shape. There were definite things that she needed to do, and there were a lot of them. Her life was changing rapidly.

At first, we worried about being able to continue to support the initial 20 students for as long as they continued in school. We thought about the horror that would exist if we had to drop students due to a lack of funds. We thought about the cruelness of building hope for the students and their families, then not being able to follow through on our promises. Those were fears that we lived with.

However, we couldn't let those fears paralyze the work. We needed to trust that no student would be dropped due to a lack of funding. It was a step of faith. Eventually, we were able to build a buffer in our bank account to give us some breathing room during hard economic times. The fact that there were no guarantees became very real for us. It increased our determination to do our best to make this program work for the people of Villa Garcia.

As the buffer in the bank account grew, it generated somewhat of a philosophical split between the members of our group. The conflict arose over whether extra funds should be used to bring new students into the program or to help some of the most extreme cases of need in the village. Both ideas were focused on trying to do good things for the villagers.

Charity, in the form of direct handouts to those who are in desperate situations, directly touched the hearts of many of our team members. Others, while acknowledging these horrific needs, thought that education would lead to structural changes that would benefit people for the long term. Both groups held passionately to their ideas. This was a tough time for our group.

Eventually, we agreed to compromise. Some funding was given out directly to those in need. Rosalia and another lady in the village managed these funds, carefully consulting others in the village to identify those most in need. They took photos and maintained impeccable records accounting for exactly how the money was used. The majority of the extra funding was used to bring in new students and support their educational expenses.

Over the years, we have grown stronger in the direction of educational sponsorships leading to longer term improvements. This philosophical direction has become a part of our organizational objectives.

However, several of our team members have worked to support another organization in the village which does more of the direct charitable gifts. Fran and a group of local villagers do all of this work in mostly rural areas surrounding Villa Garcia. This work focuses on building relationships in addition to providing direct support. It is done outside of the formal umbrella of Weavers of Hope. Interestingly, in doing this charitable outreach work, our team in Mexico often finds excellent candidates to enter our sponsorship program. It all works together quite well.

The growing pains that we were experiencing finally reached the breaking point a few months later as we prepared to add a new group of students and sponsors.

Two friends of Fran, Pearl and Alicia, were running a non-profit organization. As a way of supporting us, they allowed our donors to support the students in Villa Garcia by contributing to a special project within their organization. In the end, it was not a viable solution. It was time for a full scale review of everything.

There were so many forces converging on our work that it became very obvious that we needed to move in a direction which would be sustainable over the long term. It was almost a relief to know this with such clarity. We filed the paperwork to become a licensed corporation in the state of Texas. Our name would be Weavers of Hope. That name would honor the several hundred year old tradition of weaving in Villa Garcia.

Rebecca, the attorney who led the fight against the crooked land developers in the *colonias* of Rio Grande City, Texas, would be a member of our Board of Directors, and advise us on the legal ramifications of incorporation. She would provide this service *pro bono,* for free, because she believed in our cause. She is also a sponsor for the students in Villa Garcia.

The other person who was instrumental in helping us at this time was our friend and Certified Public Accountant (CPA), Van. The Internal Revenue Service (IRS) requires that an organization go through a very rigorous process to receive its recognition of exemption. This is commonly called a 501(c)(3) status, as that is the section of tax law which covers this type of organization. This certification allowed our sponsors and donors to write off their contributions as charitable deductions when they filed their annual tax returns.

The form was lengthy and technically challenging to complete. Van dedicated countless hours working with me on this process. He stressed the importance of obtaining IRS acceptance with the first submission of the form. We worked diligently to accomplish that, being thorough and specific on every point on the form. When in doubt, we went to the extra work of providing more detail. We passed on the initial submission to the IRS. I am still thankful to Van for all of his efforts on that work. His knowledge and insights allowed this to succeed.

Van is another one of my heroes. I met him a few years after my retirement from my computer job. During that time of transition in my life, I did seasonal tax work for three years. The last year was with a small CPA firm where Van was employed. We became friends almost immediately. I was the new, part-time, non-accountant in the firm, but you would have never known it. I was warmly welcomed by all of the staff, perhaps even more so by Van. His knowledge and skills were obvious. But, what I noticed even more was his sincerity and caring with everyone he dealt with. He treated the CEO of the firm and the janitorial staff with exactly the same kindness.

I had the opportunity to work with Van more closely on a couple of audits in Austin. He did all of the technical work related to the audit, and I got to be his helper. Working with Van was fun. He explained things well, and was very patient with me. He was also generous in offering positive feedback. He made me feel valuable and appreciated. Seeing his relationships with the clients reinforced my earlier impressions of his sincerity and kindness.

This was a man I liked and respected. Plus, it was fun hanging out with Van. As part of our audit planning, we would review the restaurant possibilities for that part of town. We both liked to eat and to plan our lunch spots. It was one of the little side treats of the day.

I would later see an even deeper level of love and loyalty in Van when his beloved wife, Lynn, experienced health problems. By that time, he had opened his own small CPA firm and was dealing with the job pressures of going out on his own. He made Lynn's care priority number one, and brought work home so that he could be with her as he worked late into the nights. He never complained or griped. He did everything with love. What a great example! Eight years later, Van is still our CPA for Weavers of Hope. He has never charged us a penny for his many hours of work. Van and Lynn are our wonderful friends. He continues to be a role model in my life.

So, this is where it all began, crossing geographical and personal borders. I have no idea where it is all going, just as I didn't in 2002, when we first contacted Fran. Like her, I trust that everything will work out OK. I believe that I'll be able to accept whatever happens, and at the same time, I open myself up to all of the possibilities that lie ahead. My hopes and dreams are immense.

> *"They are forever free who have broken*
> *Out of the ego cage of I and mine*
> *To be united with the Lord of Love.*
> *This is the supreme state.*
> *Attain thou this and pass from death to immortality."*
>
> — **Bhagavad Gita (second chapter)**

## Fran

The five-year-old child was both ordinary and mystical. How could one so young sense a calling to another place, a different culture, a country she did not know existed? Mexico was already in her heart. These intuitive feelings went beyond the visible, tangible world of her childhood. They put her in a different dimension, one that she accepted freely and without notice. What else would a five-year-old do? Innocence and openness were inherent to her. Her childhood fascination with things and feelings moved easily from one experience to the next. It would take years before she could look back on these times and feel the mysticism of what took root in her in these early years.

For Fran, the Mexican people would be woven throughout the events of her life. Their culture, language, and struggles would become a part of her and help to shape the woman she would become. Eventually, she would live in central Mexico in the village of Villa Garcia in the state of Zacatecas. The people of the community would embrace her. She would also be the cornerstone for Weavers of Hope, a non-profit organization dedicated to improving lives through education. Yet, Fran would retain her identity as a North American, a mid-western farm girl who grew up and chose to be immersed in the lives of others. Her calling was to a life of service, grounded in a deep spirituality.

Fran grew up as one of twelve siblings on a farm in Peru, Ohio. Peru is in northern Ohio between Toledo and Columbus. As a child, she felt the love of her parents, Clemens and Blandina (called Blondie by her friends), as well as their German predisposition toward hard work and discipline.

She rose with the other children at 5 a.m. to begin the chores for the day. While the boys went with their dad to milk the cows, the girls tended the garden, planting and harvesting a wide variety of fruits and vegetables.

The milk was sold, and the eggs were traded in town for various other food items. After the sales and bartering, there was seldom a need to buy other groceries. The basement rooms in the farm house were always busy. That was mission control for the canning operation, providing food for the winter months. There was constant traffic to the potato cellar, which also housed the apples. In keeping with their German food traditions, the family made their own sauerkraut. However, they broke from their German roots and made wine instead of beer.

The sudden jolt of Blondie's mental illness changed everything. The doctors surmised that an earlier bout with rheumatic fever may have caused the mental problems. However, regardless of the source, Blondie's instability emerged abruptly and traumatized the family. Her condition made it hard to keep the large family functioning. Things would never quite be the same after that.

Then, when it seemed like things were stretched to the breaking point, it got worse. The birth of Fran's younger brother, Tom, triggered severe post-natal depression in Blondie. The combination of the depression and mental illness pushed things out of control. When Blondie almost smothered Tom there was no other choice but to commit her to a mental institution. The doctors told her that she should not have any more children. She had six more.

When Blondie returned home, six months later, she was much better, but not fully cured. She was often bed-ridden. Fran was relieved to see the improvement, yet still cautious and leery of what could be. The older children took turns staying home from school to care for her.

As a first grader, Fran was sent to an aunt's home so that she could catch the school bus from there. The job of acquainting her to school and the outhouses was left to her older brothers.

When Blondie was functioning reasonably well she was able to do things around the house. She wrote lists of chores for the children to do. Fran was nine years old when she became one of her mother's care takers.

Occasionally, Blondie dropped out of reality, and things got more bizarre. Once, when the children brought her the medications she needed, she jumped out of bed and fled. She was running through the house, jumping over beds, and yelling to get away from the children. This sent shivers of fear running through Fran and her siblings. Where would this behavior end? Would she again try to harm one of the children? No one was sure after what happened with Tom.

Fran's dad, Clemens, worked hard to keep things from completely disintegrating. He succeeded. He dedicated himself to searching for adult supervision for his children, feeling strongly that it was important. For the most part, the children rose to the occasion, accepted their jobs, and kept the household functioning. Since the children had limited life experiences, they often didn't realize how dysfunctional Blondie's behavior really was.

If there was ever a spare moment for Clemens to enjoy, he would immerse himself in his shop where he did metal sculpturing and woodworking. To this day, Fran proudly displays a candle holder and fruit bowl that he crafted.

The religious values which dominated Fran's life came from both of her parents. On Friday nights, Fran would ride with her dad to special church services where they prayed for the troops in Korea, singing hymns on the way. Her mom, who had wanted to be a nun, listened to religious services of all denominations on the radio. Her angel food cakes were the hit of the church socials.

Six of the twelve children entered the religious life, although only Fran and one sister would take their final vows. In sixth grade Bible history class Fran felt her personal call to the religious life. This inspiration surfaced during a class on Mary. Blondie was very pleased with the vocational choices of her children. Clemens was more cautious and practical by nature, but he gave each child his blessing, including Fran.

At the age of 60, Blondie was rushed to the hospital. The doctors believed that blood clots broke loose and caused the heart attack which took her life. The last several years of Blondie's life were joyous, and she was in good health, both mentally and physically. Fran observed how differently she raised the younger children, being less rigid and conforming. Perhaps, with her mental illness and raising 12 children, she learned the importance of letting go of the little things and picking her spots to guide and discipline.

At the tender age of 13, Fran entered the prep school which trained "little nuns" to enter the convent three years later. Discipline and obedience were key components of the training. These "little nuns" got up early to pray, meditate, and attend Mass before their academic classes began. They did a variety of service projects, including visiting senior citizens and bringing them their food trays.

Fran was usually very obedient and complied with the disciplinary rules, but not always. Her radical side began to show itself when her junior professed mistress asked each sister to write a paper about the faults and shortcomings of their fellow classmates. Fran refused. The assignment contradicted what she felt was ethical and moral. Instead, she wrote a non-accusatory poem. Somehow, the poem was accepted and the crisis eased. This would not be the last time that Fran refused to comply with requests which violated her core beliefs. She knew that there would be times when her personal convictions would trump strict, blind obedience.

Clemens and Blondie faithfully arrived to see Fran on visiting days, bringing home baked cookies and treats. Sometimes, homesickness made Fran want to bolt from the school and return to the farm with her parents. But the Sunday afternoon singing of Latin vespers and Gregorian chants, which was her favorite activity, managed to keep her from leaving.

Prep school merged into life in the convent, and the years rolled by. When the nuns in training received their habits (special nun's clothing) many of them were enamored by it. Fran thought that they were missing the point of the vocation, when they thought that the habit made them special. Fran's comment was, *"Who needs a habit to live this life?"* She tried to model herself after those of the nuns who were smart and determined, yet humble and kind. They were the ones who were not overly attached to any material things, including the habit.

Fran's pledge of obedience was tested shortly after taking final vows in her religious community. As the time for receiving her master's degree in guidance and counseling drew near, Fran was told to change her major to English. The reason was that the local Catholic high school needed an English teacher. She was very unhappy about this and asked if she might take electives in order to finish up in Guidance and Counseling. Her request was approved. The elective that she chose in "Reading Disabilities" turned out to be a tremendous help in her future teaching assignments.

Fran was learning a lot about obedience and giving up control. These were sometimes difficult challenges, especially when the instructions that she received contradicted her personal convictions. She would always pray and think carefully about these decisions. She prayed for wisdom and guidance in knowing what was the right thing to do. Often the clarity she sought emerged when she was fully involved with her other work assignments. In letting go of the struggle, she found the answer.

Fran soon found herself working in rural areas around Toledo, Ohio where there was a large migrant community. This work experience prepared her for what would come next. When her Franciscan community decided to adopt a mission, Fran was selected to go to Chiapas, Mexico. Chiapas is in the far southern part of Mexico, close to the Guatemalan border.

Fran had dreamed of doing missionary work for many years. This possibility excited her. She vaguely recollected the attractions and feelings toward Mexico from her early childhood. She thought that this was the time in her life when those early intuitions would begin to play out.

However, that was not the case. Mexico would have to wait. The diocese of Toledo was in the process of setting up a department to serve the Spanish speaking people, and they needed an assistant director. Fran was asked to take the job. She set aside her personal desires to go to Mexico and said yes to the offer, but on one condition. She asked for the same cultural and language training that the priests, who were dedicated to this ministry, were getting. It was not common for a woman in a religious order in the 1960s to be so assertive. However, this was not the first time that the leadership group had seen Fran's determination. They acquiesced to her request, and she was off to Mexico City for language school.

Mexico City would be an eye-opening experience for Fran in many ways. As a young lady in her late 20s in secular dress, travelling throughout the capital city alone, she often attracted the catcalls and whistles of the men. This made her uncomfortable, and she searched for ways to discourage the unwanted attention. She decided to flash her profession ring. This ring is given when you make your final vows, and it is worn on the wedding ring finger. The men thought that she was married and left her alone. There seemed to be a cultural boundary that existed in the male population between harassing single women and married women. Fran used this strange cultural boundary to her advantage.

Fran lived with an upper, middle class family in Mexico City. They were good, kind people and she liked staying in their home. They included her on family walks, watched TV together, and gave her good advice on a variety of topics.

However, one incident with the family did not go well. It abruptly introduced Fran to Mexico's vague sense of time. It was quite different from her German roots and convent life. When Fran was walking with the family one evening they told her that they would "be right back" to get her. She sat on the curb waiting for them. Two hours later they returned to find her in tears. It was a tough way for Fran to learn that time arrangements in Mexico had a totally different meaning than in the U.S.

With limited language skills in Spanish, Fran struggled to fit in with their family life. Marisol, their four-year-old daughter, became Fran's pal. Little Marisol would pull Fran in the direction she needed to go as the events of daily family life unfolded. She loved helping her "big sister" who spoke that other language.

Being in a large metropolitan city was intimidating in many ways. Catching the buses was a heart-in-your-mouth experience in Mexico City. People jammed onto the buses beyond what seemed possible. If you got one foot onto the bus you were in. The rest of your body often hung in space over the concrete streets as the drivers whipped their way through the city.

Public transportation was the way that almost all of the citizens navigated the capital city. Getting to and from the buses required considerable walking through the maze of streets that made up this city of some 15 million inhabitants. None of this deterred Fran. She was finally where she wanted to be, and she was learning the language that would be essential to her future.

Before completing her studies in Mexico City, Fran had the opportunity to experience one of the grandest celebrations of the Mexican culture. On December 12th visitors from all over the world converge on the Basilica of Our Lady of Guadalupe, on the outskirts of Mexico City.

According to tradition, Juan Diego, a simple Aztec Indian, was walking between his village and Mexico City when Our Lady of Guadalupe appeared to him. The date was December 12, 1531. The Virgin spoke to him in his native, Nahuatl language, and instructed him to build a church at the site of her appearance.

When Juan reported the apparition to the bishop, he was understandably skeptical. He asked Juan for something tangible to confirm the story. Juan returned to the site where the Virgin had appeared to him. She came for a second time. It was the dead of winter, but when she appeared, Spanish roses bloomed at his feet. Juan gathered them up in his apron and brought them to the bishop. As he opened his apron and the roses tumbled out, the image of the Virgin was imprinted on the cloth. It is the image of Our Lady of Guadalupe that is now so familiar throughout the world. The bishop was convinced.

He ordered the church to be built.

On the special feast day of December 12th, the religious celebrations, dances, festivals, and traditions rival those of any on the globe. The basilica is the most-visited Catholic shrine in the world. The indigenous people along with Mexican citizens embrace Our Lady of Guadalupe as the patroness of North and South America. Because of her apparition to Juan Diego, a simple indigenous man, they see her as the woman of the poor. She symbolizes hope for those who are often without hope in their lives, a bridge between rich and poor, an opportunity to live in dignity.

As Fran was immersed in the celebration, in the middle of thousands of Mexican citizens and pilgrims, she felt a strong, permeating connection to these people. Her premonitions from early childhood flashed through her mind. Like Our Lady of Guadalupe, these would be her people.

Upon returning to the U.S. from language school, Fran was anxious to put her Spanish into practical use in a way that would be helpful to the Mexican people. She spent the next month in Brownsville, Texas on the Texas-Mexico border working with migrant families. She got to know the area that Texans call "the Valley". It is a hot, dusty area with little vegetation and frequent shortages of water. It is an area where English and Spanish are frequently intermixed into what the locals call *Spanglish*. *Tex-Mex* food and Tejano music are other signs of the blended cultures.

Fran got to know how the migrants lived and saw their problems firsthand. She learned that they followed the crops, travelling to Ohio to work in the summers. They returned to Texas in the winters to harvest cotton and fruit.

Her daily life included interacting with these families, building relationships of trust, and providing much needed friendship and counseling. These experiences were both helpful for the migrants and fulfilling for Fran.

Fran would often run into the same families in both states, and they would delight in finding each other. They would visit in the shacks and barns where the migrant families lived in deplorable conditions. Rain water would leak through the cracks causing them to scramble to move their clothes and few possessions into dry areas. The cracks were a super highway for bugs and insects. Rat-infested barns added a constant sense of terror to their daily living. Some people fled to sleep in their cars and trucks to escape the haunting fear of the rats. This was their reality.

One of Fran's jobs was to translate the children's English into Spanish for their parents. The migrant farm children wanted to fit in with their English speaking peers, so they were often embarrassed to speak their native language. This added additional stress within the families as their basis for communication was slowly disappearing. The loss of culture and traditions often followed the language divide.

Fran's passion and energy for helping these migrant families was becoming the dominant theme in her life. Her mind was continually processing a multitude of ideas for how she could most help them.

Upon returning to Ohio, she took part in a Latino leadership training program. The focus was on helping people to be prepared to represent themselves. Don't do for others what they can do for themselves. That approach provided a sense of fulfillment and dignity in the Latino leaders. They would then train more people from their communities to become leaders, thus propagating a feeling of hope among people who desperately needed it. To Fran, this provided a glimpse of how education and training can change things for the long term.

In the winter months, when many of the migrants return to Texas, Fran wanted to stay involved in their lives. Because of her religious vow of obedience, Fran's Franciscan community needed to approve job changes. She wrote a job description that would allow her to travel with the migrant families between their farm work in Ohio and Texas. It was approved. Fran began the annual commute with them on the highways between the two states which connected their lives.

One glaring need that Fran clearly saw was the importance of better communications among those who worked with these families on both ends of their migratory path. These were the same people, struggling for survival in two different states. There was a need for continuity in working with them.

With education, jobs are possible. With jobs and income, people can lift themselves out of poverty, and live with a sense of dignity. Those were the foundational concepts that led Fran into pastoral work in the Brownsville migrant school. The fact that the school was dreadfully lacking in books and supplies only made her resolve stronger.

Only the migrant farm children attended this school. They were separated from the rest of the population, just as their parents were isolated in the barns and shacks. Few people were willing to acknowledge their existence. They were the hidden, forgotten part of the society.

Since the families followed the seasons of the crops, the school year did as well. The fact that it was not in synchronization with the rest of the Texas schools was of little importance to anyone. Children often had to put work in the fields ahead of their work in the classroom.

When Fran reflects back on this school, she remembers the big, first grader she taught who was 12 years old. She was a first grader who was beginning her menstrual cycle and dating. She remembers the mom who desperately needed money but was too sick to work. Fran took her place in the fields on that day. The sun blared down as the temperatures reached 100 degrees Fahrenheit. Fran was picking hot chili peppers. As she wiped the sweat from her face, she felt the sting of the chili peppers. Fran gave her day's wages to the mother who was ill.

The harshness of this life was worth it for Fran when she saw a student succeed. Rosalia was one of those students. She was a smart, motivated, spiritual young lady, who eventually graduated from the university. These kids helped Fran to remember that in the midst of the hardships, some lives were being transformed. These were the things that motivated Fran and got her out of bed each morning.

As Fran built greater levels of trust with these families, they shared more and more of their stories and problems with her. She learned of many of the horrors in their lives. As this type of information rolled out and the communications between the social workers in the two states improved, the problems began to be addressed. Slowly, there were signs of progress.

The depths of these relationships and friendships were growing. Fran was one of the few people who were with the migrants on both ends of their yearly journey. They were becoming family for each other.

Eventually, Fran decided that it was time for her to stop migrating and live exclusively in Texas. In her transient status, she was somewhat limited in being able to advocate for their needs. She was not able to vote in either state. She was ready to speak for these families at state level hearings, voice their stories, and cast her ballot. These desires would eventually lead her to settle in La Feria, Texas, about 30 miles west of Brownsville, and very close to the Mexican border. Her work with the migrant families continued for several more years in the Valley of Texas.

Fran's work assignments became more varied. She was a live-in counselor for a teenage girl's home for narcotics addicts, a teacher, and a social worker. She lived for a time in an attic room. This became her hermitage, and gave her an opportunity for extended periods of prayer, solitude, and reflection. On the hot summer nights she found her way outdoors to sleep on the cool grass.

It was a time of change for Fran. Her life had been extremely active and consuming, but she was now feeling a stronger need for times of silence and prayer. These would be trends that would continue in her throughout her life.

In the summers, when Fran was in her early 40s, she joined the United Farm Workers (UFW) boycotts. The UFW was co-founded by Caesar Chavez and Dolores Huerta. Chavez was a Mexican American farm worker, labor leader, and civil rights activist. In 1952, he was hired as a community organizer for the Community Service Organization, a Latino civil rights group.

In the mid 1960s, Chavez, Dolores Huerta, and the farm workers union led a strike of California grape pickers protesting for higher wages. The historic farm workers march went from Delano to the California state capital in Sacramento, some 340 miles. The union encouraged the American people to boycott table grapes as a show of support. The strike lasted five years and attracted national attention. Robert F. Kennedy came out in support for the striking workers. The boycott resulted in the entire California table grape industry signing a three-year collective bargaining agreement with the UFW in 1970.

Similar movements in southern Texas supported fruit workers. The strikes and boycotts eventually led to the signing of collective bargaining agreements, which led to higher wages and better overall treatment of the farm workers. Chavez's birthday, March 31, has become a state holiday in eight states, including Texas. Many parks, cultural centers, libraries, schools, and streets have been named in his honor throughout the United States.

Fran's talents and dedication while performing summer volunteer work with the UFW opened new doors for her. She was invited to become a part of a Migrant Worker Ministry within the National Farm Workers Union. She readily accepted the offer. This assignment led to an invitation to work on the national grape boycott in Inglewood, California, a rapidly growing Latino section, southwest of Los Angeles. Fran was working at the UFW headquarters there, directly with Cesar Chavez. She was gaining recognition for her dedication to the movement.

Fran worked a number of jobs there, including one as a telephone operator with one of Dolores Huerta's daughters. Dolores Huerta is considered by many to be equally important to Cesar Chavez in leading the Chicano civil rights movement. She holds a number of honorary titles, including an honorary degree from Princeton University which she received in 2006.

While working as a telephone operator for the UFW, Fran placed calls from Chavez to President Jimmy Carter at the White House. The significance of the Chicano civil rights movement was historic, and in a small way Fran was in the middle of this work. The little girl from Ohio was on the national stage.

On days off Fran released the job tensions and stresses by going on hikes in the surrounding mountains. On one of these hikes, she broke her leg. She remembers not missing a day of work because of the injury. She was resilient and determined to do her part for the people she had come to love. Nothing was going to stop her.

When the Communications Department of the UFW began computerizing their efforts, Fran was asked to work in the newly forming, computer department. Initially, she was given a computer and told to learn how to use it so that she could begin training the other employees. She readily accepted the challenge, becoming so immersed in the work that she often forgot to take breaks and eat lunch. Soon, she was in charge of the department.

She found herself supervising the translation of the farm worker documents into Spanish and printing out Chavez's correspondence. At night, she took turns on the security watch with other members of the department. On Sundays there were rich, ecumenical, religious celebrations that included all faith traditions. Prayer was a significant part of the movement, perhaps the part that allowed the staff to continue on under such demanding pressures and deadlines. The UFW work was intense, but she loved it.

Fran had always been keenly aware of the rhythms of her body and mind. Like the seasons, she recognized these changes within herself. She was respectful of these inclinations and leanings. She instinctively knew that it was going to be an upcoming season in which she would need more solitude, prayer, and peace. The intensity of the three years with the UFW came with a price tag. She sensed this and knew that it was time to leave before burnout set in.

Upon leaving the UFW, Fran's nomadic lifestyle continued. She spent the next two years in two different houses of prayer in Pennsylvania and North Carolina. It was exactly what she needed, and provided the transition for what would come next in her life. She did gardening, cooking, tended a hostel for Appalachian Trail visitors, and helped to host retreats at the prayer houses. She spent time in nature, walking, thinking, and just being. The sounds of the frogs singing in the nearby creek soothed her. God in nature has always been a calming influence in her life.

At the end of these two years, while still in her early 40s, she felt an even deeper call to quiet and solitude. This led her to a hermitage in Ava, Missouri. Her application to live there was accepted, and she ventured out to her new life with anticipation, and a little uncertainty. It was another step into significantly greater solitude and exploration of her deepest interior being.

The isolated hermitage contained six, small living spaces which were built into the hillside to take advantage of the natural cooling and heating. The concept didn't always work, especially when the summer heat was at its highest intensity. The little homes were separated by enough distance so that each person could exist without seeing their neighbors. The setting nurtured quiet and solitude. There was no stimulation from the outside world, nor was there access to radio, television, or newspapers.

The days began at 3 a.m. with private prayer in the small prayer space which was contained in each dwelling. Daily Mass followed. Then, the hermits worked for four hours each day, doing tasks to support the community. Not surprisingly, Fran chose to work in the garden where her childhood experiences on the family farm were put to good use. The beans, potatoes, tomatoes, lettuce, and other produce from the garden supplied most of the food needs for the enclave. When something else was required, there were designated members from the community who went to town to make the purchases. The other hermits, including Fran, never left the compound.

Cooking was done by each person in their private living area. Fran used a hot plate and small toaster/broiler oven to prepare her meals. On Sunday the hermits gathered together to prepare and eat a common meal. This was their only communal time except for monthly meetings which were used to cover the business of the community. It was intended to be a very simple life, and it was.

The hermits were also required to learn an income producing trade to help support the community. Fran learned to weave. She loved to design the patterns and choose the colors. She made placemats and the stoles which are worn by priests for liturgical celebrations. Both were good sellers.

The change of pace from the pressures of the UFW years allowed Fran's body and psyche to slow down and settle. She experienced a deep peace at the hermitage, except for one thing – the crazy one.

Sr. Ann, one of the founders of the hermitage, was schizophrenic. She was institutionalized for some time, but returned to the hermitage more mentally unstable than ever. When her dark side came out, she was angry and violent.

One of the hermits worked in the greenhouse. Instead of thinning the plants, as instructed, she pulled all of them out of the ground and replanted a few of them. When Sr. Ann discovered her error, she flew into a rage, picked up a knife, and began chasing the terrified hermit. Thank God, Sr. Ann was not a fast runner.

On another occasion, in the dead of winter, Fran put a log into the pot-bellied stove for warmth. Sr. Ann thought that it was an unnecessary indulgence. She picked up the lit log and began chasing Fran with it. The hermits lived in constant fear of her violence and eruptions.

Sr. Ann wasn't always violent. She could also be funny, in an eerie sort of way. Once, in a group sharing meeting, she stuffed a dishcloth into her mouth so that she would not verbally abuse anyone. As the meeting went on, she sat there with the rag literally hanging out of her mouth, and her wild eyes covering every face in the room. The hermits watched her carefully for signs of another outburst. They weren't sure whether to laugh, cry, or run.

At the end of three plus years in the hermitage, without ever leaving the compound, Fran again noticed the seeds of change growing within her. She knew that quiet and solitude would always be a major part of any lifestyle that she chose. At the same time, the call to a more active life was luring her back into traditional society.

Fran left the hermitage with good feelings and the determination to hold on to the times of quiet and solitude. She decided to enter a monastery in Parkersburg, West Virginia where she taught classes. Fran began to find a comfortable balance of quiet time, prayer, and an active life. During these years, she helped a student named Julieta with her reading. Unbeknownst to Fran, many years later Julieta would work for Fran as the first paid employee of Weavers of Hope.

At this time Fran joined a group in Parkersburg that was dedicated to working for social justice. This was something which came naturally to her after years of working on behalf of Latino civil rights. This group would meet weekly to read and discuss various issues in the social arena. Some of the members of the group, including Fran, took personal vows of nonviolence, a core teaching of Jesus, Gandhi, and Martin Luther King, Jr.

Fran's group organized the first mother-daughter Witness for Peace group to go to Nicaragua. Witness for Peace is a politically independent, national grassroots organization which functions on the principles of nonviolence. They advocate for peace, justice, and sustainable economies in the Americas. Sometimes this requires them to challenge U.S. and corporate policies which contribute to poverty and oppression. During the Contra War in Nicaragua in the 1980s they brought U.S. citizens directly into the war zones of Nicaragua to witness firsthand the effects of the U.S. government's policies.

Fran's years of work with migrant families and her efforts on the Nicaraguan project were feeding her long considered dreams of living and working abroad. She had been sponsoring an Ethiopian orphan for some time, and this led her to submit an application to teach in the orphanage where her sponsored student lived.

When the priests who were in charge saw her resume, they immediately asked her to teach philosophy in their seminary in Addis Ababa, the capital city. That was not to be, however, as she could not get a visa. Ethiopia was ruled by Mengistu, the most prominent officer of the Communist military junta. He didn't want religious, women, or educators entering the country. Fran fit all three categories.

Later, Fran lived alone in a poor neighborhood in Parkersburg, West Virginia. As an AmeriCorps VISTA volunteer, she began training others to teach ESL in the evenings, after her classroom work was finished. She felt that this would be the right time for her to complete work on a permanent teaching certificate. It would offer her some future security and continue to open doors for potential employment opportunities.

Fran began teaching at Saint Mary's Catholic School and took courses toward a second master's degree. Over the next five years at Saint Mary's she accomplished her goal and received her permanent teaching certificate. She fell a few courses short of completing her second master's degree. However, the master's program allowed her to spend a summer in Ecuador with the help of a special grant from Boston College. The people of Latin America continued to be a major part of her life.

When Fran was in her late 50s, her dad was beginning to experience failing health, so she took a pastoral job with the Mercy Migrant School where she could be closer to him. She divided her time between Ohio and Florida. The Ohio time would put her in close proximity to her father's home, and allow her to spend considerable time with him.

In addition to her pastoral duties, Fran helped a group of Latino adults who were studying for their citizenship test. Many of them had waited years for the opportunity to become U.S. citizens, and this test would be a major milestone in their lives. Citizenship, like the birth of a child, was an event that many of them held close to their hearts. Fran felt their excitement and shared in their joy when the swearing in ceremony finally arrived.

Fran also did a variety of other tasks during this time period, including visiting the sick, cooking meals for school children, keeping order on the playground, and providing rides for children who were not able to ride the school bus.

While working on the Florida end of this job, Fran met Kiko, Rosalia, and their children. This family would provide the personal connection which would change Fran's life and fulfill her earliest childhood inclinations. The family was living with Kiko's sister, Carmen, and her husband, Gustavo. Kiko was working on his master's degree and writing a book on weaving and the generational tradition of this craft in his village, Villa Garcia.

Fran was visiting two of her sister friends, Pearl and Alicia. They were running *Centro Campesino,* Farmworker Center. Kiko, Rosalia, Carmen, and Gustavo were volunteers at the center. A friendship developed, and when everyone learned that Fran was also a weaver, there was much common ground for discussion. Kiko visited Fran's workshop, inspected her loom, and the two began exploring opportunities to market the weavings from Villa Garcia in the U.S. Fran would join Kiko's family for various outings and social interactions.

In 1998 Kiko and Rosalia invited Fran to join them when they returned to Mexico. Kiko hoped that Fran would work with the weavers in Villa Garcia and help them to find markets in the U.S. to sell their products. Over the years Fran had turned down other offers to live and work in Mexico, but she knew that this was the right time and place.

Fran being a weaver herself, and the fact that Villa Garcia had been a village of weavers for hundreds of years seemed more than coincidental. Fran said,

> "How one can be so certain about an international move is a mystery to me, but my gut knew without a doubt. I have a strong intuition. I didn't always pay attention to it out of fear and non-recognition of its benefits. It was as if I could see around the corner and into the future. I would know when to wait or when to act, without knowing what the actual outcome would be."

Nonetheless, Fran made a three-week solitary retreat before agreeing to move to Mexico. Her gut feeling was right on target, and at the end of the three weeks Fran was more sure than ever that this was the right move for her. It was the call she heard when she was five years old, only at this time she was 60.

Years later, through Weavers of Hope, locally woven products would be sold to help sustain the weavers and the educational sponsorship program. Thus, a small part of Kiko's dream has come true.

What prompted the move from Florida to Mexico was the completion of Kiko's master's degree program in Florida. He had been offered a scholarship to continue his studies toward a doctorate degree at the University of Chapingo, approximately an hour's drive from Mexico City. The university, located in the city of Texcoco, is a federally funded public institution of higher education. Many of their programs are related to agriculture, forestry, and fishing. Kiko's expertise was in agriculture, with an emphasis on irrigation systems.

The main attraction for visitors to the university is the murals. In the old, hacienda chapel is a mural by Diego Rivera, the world renowned Mexican artist and muralist. It is called *Tierra Fecunda,* Fertile Land. This huge work, which is divided into three panels, took Rivera three years to complete. The left panel depicts man's struggle to have land. The right panel shows the evolution of Mother Nature. The center panel, connecting the two, shows the communion between man and earth. It is considered to be one of Rivera's best works.

The pilgrimage from Florida ended up at the family home of Kiko's mother in Villa Garcia, Zacatecas. The family celebrations were the beginning of Fran's early days in Villa Garcia. There was so much to celebrate – the successful completion of Kiko's master's degree, the new visitor, Fran, and the reuniting of the family. However, like in many families, the grandchildren, Fany and Ariana (Beto was still a twinkle in his parent's eyes), were the focal point of the attention.

After a ten-day visit in Villa Garcia, it was time for Kiko, Rosalia, the children, and Fran to head for Texcoco so that Kiko could begin classes. Kiko helped Fran to find work at a bilingual school for secretaries in Texcoco. All the years of ESL experience would pay dividends for Fran here in Mexico.

Within two weeks of their arrival in Texcoco, the family received the tragic news that Kiko's mother had suffered a fatal heart attack. Kiko and his family returned to Villa Garcia for the funeral, and Fran stayed on alone in Texcoco. Those were days of discovery for her as she figured out how to navigate on public transportation between where they were living and her teaching job. She was alone, in many ways.

When Kiko's family returned to Texcoco, life in Mexico began to assume some semblance of normality. Fran continued with her ESL work, expanding it to include conversation groups, individual tutoring, and helping students to do research projects. In her spare time, Fran worked on her loom, weaving new designs and making curtains for the apartment where they were living.

Everyone slept on the floor, as there was no furniture, nor the money to buy it.

After several months in Texcoco, Kiko decided that his brothers needed Rosalia and Fran to return to live in the family home in Villa Garcia. Often in Mexico, under the machismo influences of the culture, major decisions were made by the male. Kiko was no exception to this tradition. After the move, he returned to Villa Garcia on many weekends to be with his family.

Upon arriving in Villa Garcia, Fran began tutoring ESL and looking for a place to live apart from the family. She often wondered what she was doing there, but knew that this was where she was meant to be.

In 2002 the principal reservoir for the village of Villa Garcia burst, flooding the village. Fran wrote to everyone on her e-mail list asking for possible projects to help the people get back on their feet. This required her to go to Aguascalientes, a large city about an hour's bus ride from Villa Garcia, to use the internet. At that time internet service was basically non-existent in Villa Garcia.

Several responses came in. One was from a gynecologist in the U.S. who needed booties for women when they came for their check-ups. Others sent donations. The most significant and lasting response came from Fran's friend, Carol, in Austin, Texas. She was facilitating a course in JustFaith, and suggested that the participants come see for themselves what had happened and how they could best help.

When everyone agreed that education and student sponsorship would be the top priority, Fran began to see how her life's experiences were coming together. For years she'd worked with students of all ages, teaching a variety of courses along with being a certified ESL teacher. She also worked with adults who were preparing for citizenship. She knew how important it was to get an education, even more so in Mexico, where the school system seemed so fragile.

Day after day Fran watched as the buses picked up the young people to work in the factories. She wept. After reaching their mid thirties, they were often fired from their jobs and replaced by younger, faster workers who worked for less money.

Fran wondered what these folks would do after they were fired. They were not prepared for anything else, and often their bodies were ruined from the long days of standing. A twelve-hour workday was not unusual. She longed for these young people to find a way out of this dilemma. She also learned how hard it was for the rural children to go to the university. Priority was given to those who lived close to the university and to those with political contacts.

As for the weavers, their markets were being lost to countries with cheaper labor. The weavers weren't making enough to live on. Many of them were leaving their jobs and opting for work in the factories. Abandoned looms, covered in cobwebs, marked the loss of a way of life. The long tradition of weaving in Villa Garcia was on the verge of collapse. It was hard for the people to keep their children in school with the meager salaries they received in the factories.

This was a perfect time to begin helping worthy students to continue with their education. Fran had been teaching English and knew many students who had no money to pay for classes. Many of them composed the nucleus of the first group of students to enter the Weavers of Hope sponsorship program.

There was Maria, Abel and Consuelo's daughter, who won various academic contests in school but wasn't given recognition. A school principal's child got the award instead of Maria. This seemed to happen over and over with the poor. There was Liliana who was fighting typhoid fever after the flood. There was Yolanda whose father was an alcoholic. There was Maria Elena whose house was ruined by the flood. There were Armando and Karen whose father stayed in the U.S., remarried there, and abandoned his family. There was Eliseo who was born with deformed arms and legs. The list goes on and on. There were so many students like these who came in and out of Fran's life, and left their marks on her soul. It was with students such as these that Weavers of Hope began.

Life among the poor in Mexico is similar to a life of poverty anywhere. Often one child would leave school so another could continue. The parents would make huge sacrifices to keep their children in school. Meals would be reduced. Living off the desert cactus when in season or off the fruit of trees if these are available or growing a few beans and a little corn if from the farm, these are their means of survival.

In the semi-desert area of Villa Garcia, Zacatecas, lack of water is a daily experience. When Fran first arrived the people were experiencing a seven year drought. Also, at that time the North American Free Trade Agreement (NAFTA) was being implemented. The farmers, who were previously able to sell crops, now were without markets and a source of income.

Nearly all rural families grow up without the use of a bathroom. They may or may not have running water, and some, even in the village, live without electricity. Most purchase potable water or get it from a spring. Clothes are washed in the stream when there is water there and hung on the bushes to dry. Farming is done with the help of horses, donkeys, and sometimes oxen.

A common occupation in this part of Mexico is brick making. Besides earth and sand, the cactus and cow manure is used to strengthen the bricks. Those who don't have ovens in which to bake the bricks make adobe. Almost all of the homes are built with brick or adobe. Even the roofs are most often of brick, and if this is unaffordable, aluminum siding is used.

Fran's living arrangements have been different and often challenging. In her first rented room she had a shower but no hot water. In the mornings, she would put a bucket of water outside in the sun and cover it with a black bag. When she returned in the evening, the water was so hot that she had to dilute it! Solar heating, in this crude form, worked well for her.

In another place Fran had a narrow bed on one side of the room and her kitchen on the other, a common occurrence in Mexico where there aren't enough rooms to accommodate all of the family members. In every case she had to go outdoors to use the bathroom.

One year in Villa Garcia, Fran was asked to work with the assistant priest. She was able to live in a dormitory room with other beds and a computer. Often, when she returned to the house, some young person would be on the computer and she could not retire. Other times two young women who would come to visit and help around the house would be asleep in her single bed. Eventually, when this happened more and more, she decided to sleep on the floor. This was not uncommon in Mexico.

The last place where Fran lived in Villa Garcia was also used as a classroom for her English classes. Kiko had built Fran a narrow bed so that it would fit in the room, along with two tables for the students. Fran fixed up the entry way with another table. She had a young woman helping to teach the classes for the younger students.

In this home, her bathroom consisted of a toilet in the middle of the patio, nothing else, not even walls. Kiko helped her to put up walls, as the children often needed to use the toilet and the temporary props kept falling down. The children didn't like the lack of privacy. Neither did Fran. She had to take a bath with water in a bucket, a feat always precarious, as she never knew when her assistant teacher would come in.

While living in that home, Fran cooked on a single hot plate using electricity. When the power went off, she had no way of cooking. She had to buy food for the day, as there was no refrigerator. The summers get very hot in this part of Mexico, and Fran's room had a wall of windows where the sunlight entered in the hot months. In the cold months no sunlight entered. It was exactly the wrong design to take advantage of the sun's natural heating.

For two years, Fran lived in the city of Aguascalientes for four days, and for three days in Villa Garcia. Crowded, shared rooms and noise were common in the city.

In 2002, Fran's 93-year-old dad, whose health had been declining, had a fall while he was on vacation with her brother. Fran went to be with him in Ohio. He died seven weeks later, and she returned to Mexico, thankful for having had those last weeks with him.

While with her dad, Fran sensed that it was time for her to have a home, and that Villa Garcia was where it should be. She wanted some permanence and stability, a place where she could set down roots. There would be no more going back and forth to Aguascalientes every week. Shortly after making these decisions, Fran's dad died. It was May 22, 2002.

The flood occurred in August of that same year. Fortunately, Fran found a piece of land to build on that was a couple of miles outside of the village of Villa Garcia. The flood did not affect construction. She was able to move there in April 2003, despite the fact that the roof was not finished and there was no operational bathroom. After years of having to go outside to use the bathroom, this was no change for her. She wanted to spend the remainder of Holy Week, the week before Easter, in her home.

When Carol and the JustFaith group in Austin had come in February of 2003, they asked Fran if she had any special needs. She needed a vehicle. She'd been walking and riding a bicycle, but for the distances now required for the work, she needed better transportation. The Austin group found a person who was willing to donate an old truck to Fran. With that truck she was able to get from her home to the students and families who needed her.

When Fran's dad died, he left each of the twelve siblings a good amount of money. With this Fran was able to finish her house, and begin building a hospitality/retreat center. The center is now known as Casa Clemens in honor of Clemens Smith, Fran's dad.

Fran continues to be the heart and soul of Weavers of Hope. Over the years, she has learned a lot about giving up control. She has immersed her total being into the people and the work that is in front of her. Living in the "now" has been something that she tries to do each day. When she does that, everything seems to work out well. Her childhood inklings about Mexico have come to fruition. She is at home with her people.

*"By detachment I mean that you must not worry whether the desired result follows from your action or not, so long as your motive is pure, your means correct. Really, it means that things will come right in the end if you take care of the means and leave the rest to Him."*

**Gandhi**

# Maria

The brown, little hands squeezed tightly around her mother's blue-jeaned legs. Two large, brown eyes peeked around that sturdy leg with curiosity, uncertainty, and a touch of fear. How safe to have that secure leg to hold on to. As my eyes caught hers, I let go with a full faced, broad smile, and she darted behind that leg for safety. Then we repeated the ritual and she held the gaze a moment longer.

Throughout my conversation with her parents, we played this little peek-a-boo gaze, smile, hide game. Eventually she was able to venture out from the leg. Our friendship was beginning, or so I thought, until she broke out into tears racing back into her mother's arms. It would take years before we could gaze openly at each other without causing her tears to flow. Hugs were out of the question. Trust is a very slow process in the Mexican culture.

After the long drive to Villa Garcia with Kiko escorting us, this would be my first night in Mexico with Abel's family. The conversation was flying fast and furious with no regard to the fact that my Spanish language abilities were pretty raw. I was grabbing onto occasional words and clinging to them like a drowning person holding onto a tree limb. It was like a word game where you try to piece together the meaning of the conversation from only a few clues. My brain was racing, so it was somewhat of a relief to play the cat and mouse game with the little girl. It was a brief pause from the mental intensity of trying to remain in the conversation. I wanted very much to connect with this family.

Nine of us had travelled from Austin, Texas to the small pueblo of Villa Garcia. We were all members of an intensive, 30-week class on social justice issues called JustFaith. We wanted to meet the people who lived here, and talk with them about their dreams and hopes for the future.

The flood which had hit this community several months earlier was now evident only in the water lines that existed on many of the adobe structures that stood close to the canal, which ran directly through the village. There was much for us to learn and do in our time in this community.

We were split up into five homes, which provided us with our lodging, food, and a sense of belonging while we were here. Then, during the days, we would join ranks and visit many other families. We all noticed a tremendous sense of warmth and friendliness toward us by our host families. This welcoming attitude extended over to the other families we visited.

Mexico tends to be a patriarchal society, but that does not necessarily imply a lack of respect between the father and mother. Their roles are often more traditional than what I am used to, but it seems very natural and easy in their culture, not like a power struggle or source of resentment. This was very much the case in the home where I was staying. The parents, Abel and Consuelo, obviously liked each other. I could see a sparkle in their eyes, almost like their own little secret, as we talked and shared stories. Seven of their eight children still lived in the family home, along with one grandson. I immediately liked the feelings of being with this family.

Abel was very patient with me, repeating things, slowing down, and waiting for me to understand. He had a lot to say, but had all the time in the world to say it and re-say it until I showed some glimmer of understanding. But then, if it looked like I understood, he opened the floodgates and his words rushed out without constraint.

Consuelo had no concept of slowing down or repeating. She was full speed ahead, speaking in rapid fire with a liberal dose of colloquialisms and an exuberant laugh that filled the room. Her joy for life was abundant and overflowing. Tough living conditions and hard work did nothing to reduce her zest for embracing this moment of social encounter. She was going to enjoy it to the fullest, a character trait which I sensed flowed over into every part of her life. The fact that I had no idea what she was saying seemed to be of no importance. My smile, presence, and attention were all that she required.

The little girl who I played peek-a-boo with had an older brother and more sisters than I could keep up with. The children flowed in and out of the room to meet me, say hello, and scope out the situation. Their curiosity was no less than their little sister's, but without the need for the blue-jeaned, security leg. They helped their mom with the food preparation, and laughed at her abundant, corny jokes and comments.

Consuelo's silliness allowed everyone to relax. She had a contagious, compelling presence. The kids carried the food and drinks to the table, cautiously observing this strange man with the white face, as if he were the first one they had ever seen, although I thought that was probably not the case.

I learned on this first night that tortillas and beans would be served with every meal that I would eat in this village. It was almost like having salt and pepper on the table. In some cases it was the main course, but not for this meal. Tonight, they had rolled out their finest cuisine for their guest.

As the food was put on the table the flies appeared. They circled over the food, and eyed their path of descent. I suppose that they didn't want to be left out from the feast that covered the table. I noticed how nonchalant the family was as they waved their hands over the food in an almost ritualistic manner to keep the flies from landing. I quickly adopted that policy, and the conversation continued amidst the flies, the waving hands, and the two big brown eyes that continued to watch me.

When it was finally time for bed, exhaustion had set in. A 20-hour drive, followed by a conversation in another language, the social pressures of trying to fit in, and a very full stomach had me craving my bed. It sounded like Abel and I would be sharing a bedroom for the next few days, but I was never sure if I was getting the messages correctly.

As Abel and I walked out of the kitchen, he led me out of the home and down a dirt path to an adobe building. The moon and stars provided our only light, but it was sufficient. There were no other homes to be seen, only the countryside. The crickets provided the musical backdrop for our walk.

As we entered the adobe building my eyes scanned my new home for the next few days. I quickly took in the surroundings. There was a single light bulb in the little mini kitchen which provided a dull glow into the bedroom. There were no other rooms. The bedroom contained a double bed, a couple of pieces of well-used furniture, and an old couch.

My mind raced ahead. Oh my God, was I going to have to share a double bed with a strange Mexican man for four nights. Panic set in. I was not ready for this, regardless of what their culture might find normal. I also had no idea how I could do anything about it. Then, he graciously used his sign language to augment the words, and indicated that the bed was for me. He would take the couch. Relief was joined by embarrassment. I was touched by the simple generosity of this man and this family. I was their honored guest. I felt cherished.

It was 2003 and a cold February night in Villa Garcia, Zacatecas, Mexico. The village is located in a high desert, with surrounding hills and mesas, lots of cacti, and few trees. They had spoken at dinner about the flood that occurred in the summer of the prior year. Without warning, the earthen dam that held the mountain reservoir above town broke. Water was dangerously close to their little home, but many other homes in the village were not so lucky. The flood took two lives, injured several, and wreaked damage on about a fourth of the homes in the village, some extensively.

Before going to bed, I grabbed my jacket and hat and went outside in search of the outhouse. There was none. Just find yourself a spot in the field where you are comfortable, if that is possible for someone from such a different life situation, and do what comes naturally. As I stood there in the cold, I wondered how many other surprises I would find tomorrow. Snuggling under a mound of woolen blankets, I burrowed in, pulling the warmth up all around me. I felt safe and secure before passing out into another world.

My first morning in Mexico was sunny and cold as Abel and I wandered back down the dirt path to the main home. I looked around more closely, trying to figure out how many rooms there were, and how they handled the sleeping arrangements for a family of nine.

Like many Mexican homes, a courtyard was in the center. It had uneven, dirt floors, as did the home. Plants of all sizes covered the patio in old, semi-rusted out cans and containers of many shapes. The family bird, which I learned was the most common pet in Mexico, sang cheerfully at the new day's unveiling. It seemed like many things were reused as part of their daily living arrangements.

The kitchen had an old, but fully functioning gas stove, and I noticed that there was a small hole in the ceiling above the stove which served as a vent. There was a simple wooden table and 6 chairs in the kitchen. Religious pictures, icons, and crucifixes adorned the walls, along with a few family pictures.

Abel and Consuelo appeared as two, beautiful, young people in their wedding photograph. The years of working in the sun had added wrinkles beyond their years to their faces, but their eyes shone with a brightness that was inviting, almost compelling.

The family either ate in shifts or used the floor to supplement the seating.

Regardless, everyone seemed very comfortable in the surroundings. The new day began with the waving ritual over breakfast. There were not as many flies as last night. Perhaps they had disbursed during the cold night when there was no food to hover over.

Consuelo proudly took us outside to demonstrate her corn-grinding stone which produced some top-of-the-line tortillas. For breakfast, she finely chopped nopalito cactus leaves and sautéed them with tomatoes, onions, and peppers, before adding the eggs to complete the omelet. The beans were already on the table in a large bowl with a serving spoon.

All of the breakfast ingredients came from their garden and their chickens. The children had a major part in the harvesting, along with a variety of other chores around the house and on the farm. When the tortillas came out of the frying pan, they immediately went into cloth embroidered napkins which were passed around for serving. The warmth penetrated the cloth and felt good on my hands as I took a generous amount of tortillas.

While we ate, Consuelo demonstrated several finished pieces of embroidery that she had done, almost like an itinerate salesperson. She seemed to want approval and recognition for her work, like artists showing off their creations. She told me that the detailed needlework was done in spite of some deteriorating cataracts on her eyes, for which there was no money for surgery. She laughed as a way of ignoring the hard facts, but I suspected that the pain was not too far below her cheerful presence.

It looked like there were two other rooms, but both had old pieces of fabric over the door, so that I couldn't see in. I guessed that they were bedrooms. Counting the bedroom where Abel and I stayed, that would make three. I was to learn that other families in the village had nine people in one room. I continued looking for a bathroom, but couldn't find one either inside or outside. It was one thing to have the privacy of darkness, but quite another in the sunshine of a bright new day.

Behind the home were goats, sheep, a large, outdoor oven where Abel earned his living making bricks, chickens, two puppies, very small fruit trees and a field which looked like it was ready for planting. Lavender, mauve, and azure-tinted clouds hung over the large rocky hills surrounding the home. There appeared to be flat plateaus on the top. There was little vegetation other than cacti on the hills. Still, no other homes were in sight. It was a very peaceful, country setting.

After breakfast I joined Abel to see how this brick-making process worked. He described and re-described the various steps until I caught on. Communications were slightly easier on day two, as he knew a little more about the limits of my language skills, and I had a better feel for his cadence. We established the universal "time out" signal when he relapsed into rapid fire chatter. It seemed to be working reasonably well.

Abel talked of getting a special type of soil from the *presa,* the dam, above town where the rupture occurred that flooded the village. That soil is then transported to the house, by what means I have no idea, as there was no vehicle on the premise. Animal dung, cactus, and water were mixed in, and the whole concoction was mixed on the ground with a shovel, Abel working the shovel with the ease and grace of a skilled athlete.

I later learned that he had played a considerable amount of baseball in his younger days, before heading up a family of nine. Years later I would bring a bat and two balls on one of my trips. The whole family, even down to the little ones, would start an impromptu game of hitting and fielding. I would join in with them, and notice Abel's graceful athleticism.

After mixing the ingredients into a thick, mud-like composition, Abel laid out a row of prefabricated forms, and taking handfuls of the mud, compressed them evenly into the forms, smoothing out the tops, and transferring the excess to the next empty form. No gloves were used - only a trowel like instrument to smooth out the tops. All of this was done on his hands and knees. I joined in, and after 15 minutes, my back began to ache. He worked on without any signs of tiring.

After the forms were loaded and packed, they were lifted off leaving a row of perfectly shaped future bricks. Abel said that they would dry in the sunlight for several days, before being transferred to the oven for eventual firing. The village receives little rain, but when it does rain, the whole family goes into race mode in covering the bricks with large sheets of plastic. The rain would ruin the drying bricks. The high desert, with a dry, sunny climate, was the perfect location for this work.

When the oven is full, every couple of months or so, large tree trunks are hauled in, doused with a liquid fire starter like kerosene, and ignited. The firing can go on for 20-plus hours, during which time Abel is always there, adding wood to the fire, and monitoring the entire process. After firing, the bricks turn bright orange, and they are cooled and stacked in piles. They are then ready to be delivered to clients who use them in various construction projects, most typically for homes and businesses. I wondered about the demand for the bricks and the profit margin.

Abel told me that for all this work, he made the equivalent of about $120 U.S. per month. He was not the *patron,* owner of this business, but only a worker. Five years later, Abel would have an old truck for transporting the raw materials and finished products, an oven of his own, and be a small business owner. This would double his income.

Abel was always thinking, and loved to talk on a wide variety of topics. I soon realized how smart this man was, and how much he would have loved the opportunity to have gone beyond third grade. Years later, when his daughter, Maria, was excelling in mathematics and winning academic competitions, she would tell me that those abilities came from her father.

Abel's mental curiosity seemed to be unbounded, as did his understanding of so many aspects of life. He talked about the research that he was doing to find out which high schools would give Maria the best educational foundation for entering the university. That was her dream, and it was obvious that he shared it with her. He talked proudly of her straight A report cards which flowed from one year to the next, and of other academic achievements of hers.

The family had already made great financial sacrifices to help Maria's older sister to complete the university and become a certified teacher. Abel's only sadness was that she now lived about six hours away, and was seldom able to visit. The closeness of this family and the pain of them being separated was a glaring reality.

Maria would be in the first group of 20 students who would receive support a few months later from a new organization called Weavers of Hope. The name came quite naturally. Villa Garcia had a long history of weaving which spanned hundreds of years. Looms were everywhere in the village, almost like a trademark. So, the name WEAVERS popped out quite easily. The idea of the organization was to bring HOPE to deserving students and their families. All of us liked the name Weavers of Hope.

The organization would provide scholarships of $20 per month to help selected students in the village to continue their education. The money would help Maria to continue in *secondaria,* middle school. This financial support would be used for uniforms, books, fees, and other school supplies.

Several years later Maria would be getting additional scholarship money from Weavers of Hope as she entered the pre-med program in the university in Zacatecas, a large colonial city about 2 hours from Villa Garcia. Small amounts of money in Mexico, by United States standards, allow great things to happen.

Maria was friendly in the socially awkward way that a 14-year-old farm girl can be. Right from the start, her smiles and gentleness made me feel comfortable around her, but her shyness put a veil over the roses of her personality. Questions and direct interaction brought about a certain formality in her. She was more comfortable in the background, listening, observing, and taking in the lively interactions among the adults. She sometimes forgot her feelings of strangeness and giggled. Her interactions with her siblings seemed natural and easy, unlike her interactions with me.

Over the next several years I would see this shy, little girl emerge into a confident, young lady. She would make direct eye contact, flash that gentle smile, and be ready to answer questions fully, as well as to ask her own. It was like the emergence of a beautiful butterfly from the cocoon. She burst forth, blossomed into glorious color, and floated easily in the air, making others feel content as she landed in their presence to be with them.

Maria was keenly aware that her parents struggled to survive and put food on the table. She was determined not to let them down as she pursued an academic career. The life that she was choosing was very different from the one her parents were living. Nonetheless, she had great respect for them, their work ethic, and their loyalty in supporting her and their other children. Maria wanted both a career and a family. She knew that her choice would cause some level of natural separation from her family, and she dreaded that. Yet, she was confident that she would be able to handle any pressures that would arise.

After completing high school, Maria's first dream was to study mathematics and pursue a degree in physics when she entered the university. However, before making this choice, she looked into what job opportunities would be available for someone with a physics degree. She learned that jobs would be limited in this area, except for the possibility of a few teaching positions. As she thought about her life after college, she began to explore several other career paths, finally settling on going to med school.

The *University Autonoma de Zacatecas* (UAZ) is recognized as the leading institution of secondary and higher education in the state of Zacatecas. They have an excellent, competitive curriculum in medicine. This was the only university where Maria applied. She was accepted in the summer of 2006, approximately three years after my first visit to Villa Garcia.

As an 18-year-old freshman entering the university, Maria left home for the first time. She anticipated that the first year would be a time of transition, but she never imagined how tough it would really be.

In going through the process of acceptance into med school, there was one day when Maria needed to be at the university in Zacatecas at 7 a.m. She arranged a ride with a friend from Villa Garcia, so was up at 4 a.m. getting ready for the trip. When they arrived at the university, there was a crowd of students already there. Maria had to stand in line in the sun for hours, without leaving the line to eat lunch. She was afraid of losing her place in line. Many students were vying for the few slots that existed in the school of medicine.

After being accepted, Maria had to figure out where she would live. It would need to be inexpensive, as her funds were limited. Her sister invited her to live with her, and Maria readily accepted. However, the commute to school would be over an hour, and Maria had no idea how that was going to be done. But, she had a place to stay.

The home had two bedrooms and one bath. With Maria, 10 people, including three children would be living in this space. Maria would be sleeping on the floor. Zacatecas is in the mountains and the winters are very cold. Maria could imagine how cold she would be on the concrete floor. When the class schedules were settled, her first class would be at 7 a.m. She imagined getting up in the cold and dark around 5 a.m., and walking a long way to wait for a bus to go to the university. This was not the vision of college life that she had imagined.

When her classes began it was the rainy season in Zacatecas. Navigating the buses in the dark with the rain coming down was a mess. She was alone, without friends, and feeling overwhelmed. Her body hurt from sleeping on the floor, and she got sick. There was really no space for her in the house and her sister's children would get into her school papers and books. It was hard to carry all of the books and papers to school, and dangerous to leave them at the house.

After about a month of living like this, Maria went home one weekend to talk it over with her dad. They both agreed that something had to change. Shortly after that, Maria found a room to rent and was able to share it with a friend from Villa Garcia who was also in the same university. That solved a lot of the immediate problems, but it also created some new ones.

"ALONE" is a word that Maria often used to describe her first year at the university. It was a deep, pervading sense of being alone. After 18 years of living with her family, where she felt the daily love of her parents and siblings, the contrast was abrupt and difficult. Her roommate from Villa Garcia had a completely different class and work schedule, so they seldom saw each other.

Maria would come home to an empty room, make something to eat, and eat alone. Eating alone was something she had seldom done. She hated it. It made her feel isolated and despondent. It was so bad that she lost her appetite and didn't want to eat. Something had to change.

Maria desperately searched for a way out of the loneliness. She made friends with the lady who lived below them. She asked the lady if she could pay her to share the meals that she was cooking for her children. She was a kind lady, and happy to be able to help Maria. Maria would come home from school, go to her house, and the two of them would eat together and talk. Maria paid her a little for a good, home-cooked meal. More importantly, the two of them became friends. Some of the feelings of being alone were easing.

Freshman year was tough. It wasn't the classes or the work that was a problem. Maria continued to do fine in her academic work, just as she had in high school. It was being alone that was the hardest thing about going to the university.

Maria is now 21 years old and has just completed her third year of med school, still making top grades. She has many friends, both at the university and in Villa Garcia, and that sense of being alone is gone. Yet, Maria can become philosophical when she reflects on the differences between the two lives that she leads. When she is at the university, she is with physicians, teachers, and other med students. Their conversations are largely focused in that area. At home, she enjoys being with her family and talking to old friends. The conversations are very different, and she notices that. However, she is comfortable living in both worlds.

Maria is no longer the shy young girl who I first met. She has become socially comfortable, including making presentations in front of large groups of peers, parents, and other community members. She is becoming a quiet, strong leader. The smiles and gentleness are still there, eight years later, but they come from a young lady of enormous potential. Her dream is to practice medicine in her community, helping her people, and being close to her family.

One of the stories about this family that I most love is the "bathroom story". On a visit during Maria's high school years, I noticed that the family was finally building their much needed indoor bathroom. When we talked about it Abel explained that they had to stop construction for a while, until they saved up some more money. That seemed natural enough, as the culture in Mexico is that they normally do their construction in this fashion. Partially built homes exist everywhere, and rooms are added on as money becomes available. A finished project can easily span a decade or more.

As we talked more, I learned the real reason for the work stoppage. Abel and Consuelo talked of a government program that was offering a discounted price on computers for students. They decided to get Maria a computer, even though it meant putting the bathroom project on hold. The priority that this simple couple gave to the education of their children was touching.

Abel and Consuelo had only finished third grade in school. Yet, their wisdom, vision, and work ethic led them to sacrifice much in order to help secure their children's future. Eventually, the bathroom was completed, and when I used it for the first time, my mind flashed back to that first night in 2003 when I stood in the fields urinating. So much had changed, yet so much was identical to that first night.

Most of the vibrant conversations took place around the kitchen table, the family meeting room. They covered a wide range of subjects - religion, philosophy, Mexican history and culture, interpersonal relationships, family matters, tending to the gardens and animals, and on and on. Abel had both knowledge and keen insights on all of these topics. Consuelo often listened and chimed in with her special nuggets and humor as she deemed fit. Often she just ignored us and tended to the household chores.

One subject that Abel and I both enjoyed discussing was politics. These discussions really peaked in early 2006, as the Mexican presidential campaign was in full swing. Abel supported Andres Manuel Lopez Obrador, a populist beloved by Mexico's poor. He charmed voters with a mix of charisma and New Deal-style public works proposals that he promised would create jobs for millions of poor Mexicans. He further claimed that these jobs would encourage his citizens to stay home, and would stem illegal immigration to the United States.

Felipe Calderon, who eventually won the tightly contested race, was a free-trade booster who promised continuity with President Vicente Fox's policies. After the voting, both sides claimed victory. It was as close as the Bush-Gore election in 2000, but there were no hanging chads in Mexico. However, like in the U.S., it took months to finally get a resolution. It was never accepted by many of the Lopez Obrador supporters. Some things seem to be universally true without regard to national borders.

On another trip the conversation centered on Abel's thoughts of going into business for himself, and getting out from under his *patron,* boss. As he described how he could do it, I got out a pencil and paper and started scribbling notes about his thoughts and plans, asking questions, and documenting costs and potential income possibilities. Together, we poured over the details, just as we did on presidential politics, and tried to think of all the angles.

The outcome pretty much matched what was in Abel's head from the outset. What it did was allow me to catch up to him. I realized that he had thought it all through, and knew that it was a viable plan. On his kitchen table, we gave birth to what was perhaps the crudest business plan that was ever documented.

Within the next year, Abel would implement it, and make it work. He is now a small business owner, not making a lot of money, but also not working for anyone else. What scares me the most is that he is beginning to have back problems, not surprising for someone doing this type of manual labor.

Consuelo and the children help in the family business, but there are not sufficient funds to hire another laborer at this point. Abel consults with Maria about the back pain and together they explore ideas from prescription medicines, which are expensive, to natural, herbal remedies. He lives with the fear of how he will provide for his family if his back further deteriorates.

Another one of my visits occurred during a family reunion. We (there were four others travelling with me) were invited to attend the large event, which was going on out in the countryside, a couple of miles from Abel's home. The men brought barbecue pits and were gathered around them drinking beer, laughing, and talking when we arrived. The women were preparing food, serving, and making sure that everyone was taken care of. The kids were running and frolicking in the middle of all this, oblivious to anything beyond playing and having fun.

The sights, sounds, and smells were full of joy and a sense of family togetherness. The food was delicious and abundant, and we were encouraged to continue eating way beyond what our stomachs would hold. This was another one of those cross-cultural truths – the universality of food and celebration.

After eating, it was time for the teenagers to control the show. They had concocted a makeshift swing by throwing a rope over a large tree limb and somehow attaching a piece of wood for the seat. Each person was then escorted to the seat of honor amidst protest, laughter, and good-natured taunting. The person of honor was encircled by a hoard of teenagers, adults, and little kids.

Then the swinging began, going as high as was possible, and being pushed from every angle.

After a good, long ride, a chant began, *"vuelta, vuelta, vuelta......"*. I quickly learned the meaning of this as they wound the swing to maximum tightness, then began unwinding it, pushing it so fast that the circular spinning was blinding. Then, the person had to get up and walk. That was the most fun of all. It brought me back to my youth when we used to spin around, get dizzy, then stumble about as we tried to walk.

Everyone got a turn on the swing, including the grandmas, but everyone also respected the boundaries of endurance and safety for each person. The gentleness that was shown to the older ladies was both inclusive and careful. But watch out for the macho, young males. No mercy was shown to them. Each one of us got our turn too, as did the little kids. I remember feeling so included and accepted into their celebration. The color of my skin and my obvious differences from them faded, and we became one family, united in this time of laughter and celebration. Smiles still cover my face today, years later, as I think about this reunion and the feelings of inclusiveness.

Returning to Mexico to the home of Abel, Consuelo, Maria, and all of her brothers and sisters is still one of my greatest joys on these trips. We have our little rituals, like the two, giant, half gallon bottles of Coca Cola for Consuelo. This is one of her true pleasures in life, and the family usually doesn't have the extra money to buy sodas. I always show up with two bottles of "Coca", as Consuelo calls it. Her face bursts forth with this big smile, she says something crazy, then we all laugh. Once I forgot the "Coca" and received no end of teasing throughout the visit. I will never forget them again.

Maria has now moved comfortably into our conversations, and she freely shares more of her life and dreams with us. Recently, she talked about an issue which she discusses often with the other med students. Part of the Hippocratic Oath that doctors take says that they shouldn't mix their emotions with their work. She knows from firsthand experience that this is not always possible. Having worked with some cancer patients, including children, she knows that human compassion will always be a part of the equation for her. She doesn't shy away from her position. Maybe others can separate totally, but she is glad that she can't. I feel sure that she will know exactly where to draw the line in terms of separating emotions and her work. I trust her judgment.

Maria also talks about her classmates who come from middle and upper class families. Many of them enter the university with attitudes of privilege. They drink excessively, party, and don't focus on their studies. Maria knows how much her parents have sacrificed to help her to get her this far in her education. It motivates her to work hard and honor them by succeeding in her classes and in how she treats others.

In interviewing Maria for this book, we asked her what she sees in her future. She answered as follows:

*"I see a difficult road ahead, but I see myself making it. I see myself achieving my goals, then making new ones. I have never been the kind of person who has just one goal. I have always wanted it all, and gone little by little in meeting one challenge after another. I don't have a precise view of my future. I have always taken life in small parts, meeting goals one at a time, and making more as I go. I have never been the kind of person who meets one goal and then stays there. I have always wanted to continue improving. For example, I entered college wanting a degree in medicine. Now, I want more. I see myself finishing my degree, having a career, and becoming a specialist. Of course, I also want a family, a house, and all of the things that everyone dreams of. And, I see myself doing all of this. Why not? Why can't I do all of this, just like lots of other people do? I have what it takes, even if some people doubt that I can accomplish all of this. I don't agree. Why not?"*

Another question that we asked Maria was what she would like to say to all of the current Weavers of Hope sponsors and supporters, and to those who are considering becoming sponsors. She said:

*"I have been in the Weavers of Hope educational sponsorship program from the beginning, and I have seen it grow from the very start. I have seen all that it has given. I would like the sponsors to know that they are not just supporting one person who is trying to get an education. They are supporting someone who is fighting to help a lot of other people. We have people like Magda, who was one of the first Weavers of Hope students to graduate from the university with a degree in teaching special education. She is now using her degree to help lots of special needs children. So, you can see that it is not just one person who a sponsor is helping. They are helping lots of people through Magda's work. Students will get their degrees, help their families, and also help their younger brothers and sisters who are in school. The program is bearing fruit, even though the harvest is long term. We have so many professionals who have come from*

*this program. We have nurses, accountants, teachers, social workers, and engineers. The program has a great future and a great foundation. The trick is to continue to find the supporters. We all hope that the support continues."*

During the course of these eight years, I have returned to Maria's home to spend time with her and her family on over 20 occasions. The little girl who hid behind her mother's leg, no longer cries in my presence, and the siblings are no longer careful when I'm around. While I'm not quite a relative, they are very comfortable in my presence and I in theirs. We all know where we stand, what to expect of each other, and when to laugh at one of Consuelo's jokes. It is easy and comfortable for us to be together.

*"Everybody can be great. Because anybody can serve. You don't have to have a college degree to serve. You don't have to make your subject and your verb agree to serve…You don't have to know the second theory of thermodynamics in physics to serve. You only need a heart full of grace. A soul generated by love."*

**Martin Luther King, Jr.**

# *Lupe*

Unlike the garden variety buzzard, which generally scavenges for dead animals, the Mexican buzzard is also known to attack small farm animals. On this day, the buzzards that glided lower in the sky were looking for any kind of food, alive or dead. Eyeing what appeared to be an animal carcass, they descended for a closer inspection. They landed on a human corpse. It was lying beside the road in Fresnillo, Mexico.

Normally, Fresnillo was not a city that was noted for violence in the 1940s. The second largest city in the state of Zacatecas, it was the center of a rich mining area known especially for silver. For almost 100 years beginning in the late 1600s the mines were worked constantly, yielding valuable minerals. Fresnillo was a junction of rail and highway routes which provided the means for exporting the minerals. Eventually, flooding caused the mines to shut down, and the region went into an economic crisis.

Economic sustainability in Fresnillo now depends heavily on agriculture. Various crops, including corn, peppers, and tomatoes, are grown in the area. The neighboring towns and villages focus on exporting these products to other parts of Mexico and internationally.

The gruesome murder was an anomaly. The perpetrators would never be found or brought to justice. One had to wonder how much effort went into tracking them down. That would remain a mystery.

Lupe's uncle, her dad's brother, was a travelling salesman who took weavings from Villa Garcia out into the neighboring communities to sell. The woolen blankets were his top sellers. The cold winters in the mountains surrounding Villa Garcia were accentuated by the stone construction and the lack of heating in the homes. The cold penetrated the stones and they created bone-chilling, tomb-like enclosures. Everyone needed the blankets, so his small, one-man business was flourishing.

Ponchos, rugs, and wall hangings supplemented his inventory. The ponchos, like the blankets, sold well in the winter months. Warmth was a top priority, even among the poor. The rugs and wall hangings had better markets with the people who had some level of discretionary income. They were in the minority.

Eventually, the banditos took note of the success of this small, little business. They viewed the one-man operation as easy prey. The robbery and brutal murder of Lupe's uncle shocked the people in the surrounding communities. Robberies were not uncommon, but brutal murders were almost unheard of. The family members were devastated, especially Lupe's dad, who went into a state of deep depression. The loss of his brother in the grisly murder implanted a sense of fear in him. This would be one of the undercurrents that Lupe grew up with.

Lupe grew up in a family that was large, even by Mexican standards. She was the youngest of 15 children. Her family ran a small *tienda de abarrotes,* grocery store. Mexican towns, especially those that are too small for any type of supermarket, are heavily populated with these tiny stores. They are significantly smaller than the convenience stores which are attached to the gas stations in the U.S. Typically, they are about ten feet square, and have merchandise packed in at a density that is hard to fathom. Villa Garcia was the type of village that spawned these little stores.

The *tiendas de abarrotes* throughout Mexico are typically run by one family. This was the case with Lupe's family. Upon entering the store, it was easy to be overwhelmed by the variety and kaleidoscope of colors that decorated the product labels and signs. Yet, amidst the clutter, there was a feeling of coziness in the intimate little space.

There seem to be far too many of these little stores for the populations they support. However, they tend to stay in business, often passing from one generation to the next. Compared to being unemployed, any little profits which are generated help to sustain the families who own them. Other family members often work outside the store to supplement the family income.

Lupe's dad was the chief disciplinarian in their family, but both parents were actively involved in raising their children. They taught hard work, respect for others, and orderliness in the home. Lupe would grow up to teach these same values to her children.

The educational system in Mexico changed when Lupe finished third grade. Those in leadership roles were examining educational psychology and reevaluating the entire educational system. Research in math education and the history of education grew considerably in the mid 1970s, and spurred significant changes. One of those resulted in a favorable outlook on beginning co-educational schools. Boys and girls were put together in the same classroom. Lupe's parents strongly disagreed with this concept, and chose to hold their youngest daughter out of school.

Perhaps this was one way that the fear from her uncle's death, most directly impacted Lupe's life. That theory will never be proven.

Two years later, Lupe's parents finally decided that it was OK for her to attend co-educational classes. By that time it was too late. Lupe was embarrassed at being so much older than her classmates. She wanted to quit school, and her parents did nothing to stop her.

Her youngest brother, who was in the same grade with Lupe, continued his education despite the mixed gender classrooms. Over the years, Lupe would watch him progress through school, eventually receiving his engineering degree from the university. The degree helped him to find good work. Lupe was proud of her brother, but felt a deep regret that her education was cut short. She vowed to fight for the education of her children. She would succeed in keeping that vow.

Children seem to be born with an innate instinct which allows them to sense which parent they should approach for permission to do something. Almost magically they are able to figure the odds, and select the parent who is most likely to go along with their request. There was no doubt in Lupe's mind that she would talk with her mom about her first serious boyfriend, Moises. Her instinct was right. For five years, Lupe and her mom shared the secret of her courtship with Moises. It was not until the year that the couple was ready for marriage that her dad was informed of the relationship. He was less than happy.

Lupe's dad demanded that the young couple wait a month to think about their wedding. He didn't want to hear any conversation on the marriage topic during the trial period. His anger at being deceived was almost as strong as his anger about the upcoming marriage. Not too secretly or quietly, he hoped that some miraculous event would stop the ceremony.

On their wedding day, Lupe's dad was still fuming as he came in from working in the fields. His shirt was smeared with animal dung, and he refused to change clothes for the wedding. It was only after the tearful pleas of his daughter and wife that he acquiesced.

Strangely enough, something snapped in Lupe's dad's head after the ceremony. Maybe it was the legality of the marriage license. No one knew for sure. But he began to accept Moises into the family. They began to develop their own relationship. When the young couple visited, Lupe's dad would offer Moises cigarettes as his form of the Native American peace pipe. Not wanting to jeopardize the fragile relationship, the non-smoking Moises went home dizzy and nauseated after the visits. But Moises thought that it was worth it for family harmony.

On the other side of the family, Lupe got along famously with her in-laws. She bonded with her mother-in-law on their first meeting. The young newlyweds were invited to live with Moises' family, a custom that often happens in the Mexican culture. Thirty-one years later, they have expanded the house and added walls to separate the living spaces, but they are still happy living as next-door neighbors.

Moises was a serious, hardworking young man who would sometimes let off steam by going drinking with his buddies after work. The alcohol accentuated his grouchiness when he returned home. Lupe would flash a big smile at him and tell him that she had prayed all day for a cape. His face frowned, not knowing what she was talking about. Lupe grinned and said, *"All good bull fighters need a cape."* This broke the tension, and Moises laughed.

In the future when he would come home grouchy, Lupe would often pull out a cape and walk through a simulated bullfight with Moises as the bull. He couldn't help but smiling. It always changed the dynamics of the situation. Over the years, Moises has mellowed and Lupe seldom needs to pull out her cape.

Lupe and Moises have raised four adult children, three of whom have received their degrees from the university. Their youngest child, Lupita, is currently in the university and working on her degree in teaching. Lupe's vow to fight for her children's education has been fulfilled. She describes their graduation ceremonies as some of the greatest joys of her life.

Moises Junior, the oldest of the four, is married with two little girls of his own. He teaches in a rural school about two hours from Villa Garcia. Lupe pulled her daughter-in-law, Sandra, aside to advise her how to handle Moises Junior when he was in a bad mood. Lupe's advice was to walk away from him and refuse to argue. Sandra did this the next time her husband was looking for a fight. Moises Junior stormed off, slamming the door. When he returned about an hour later he was calm. He asked Sandra why she refused to talk with him. Sandra replied, *"Your mother said to ignore you because you're crazy."* He laughed at the wisdom of his mother and wife. They had him figured out before he realized that he was a problem.

Maribel, the second daughter, graduated from the university with a degree in nursing, and is currently working as a teacher in health sciences. The security of her teaching position and the benefits that the job offers have her debating on whether to pursue a career in teaching or nursing. Her education has given her the ability to choose.

The oldest daughter, Mireya, began as a Weavers of Hope scholarship student in 2006. She completed her university degree which focused on early education, including operating a day care center. She is also receiving her teacher's certification so that she has multiple options in the future, like her sister, Maribel.

Lupe and Moises worked hard all of their lives to be able to support their children's education. When they sold their *tienda de abarrotes,* Lupe's dad bought a small ranch where they raised a variety of crops, including corn, beans, squash, and peas. When the harvest was good, he had products to sell. Mireya says, *"My dad does a little bit of everything. He loves to work in the fields from morning to sundown. When he is not in the fields, he works as a brick maker and weaver. He is always busy."*

Like Lupe, Moises also supports his children's education. During the summers when Moises Junior was in school, his dad brought him to work in the fields. He taught his son to work the farm, cut wood, make bricks, and cut stone. At the end of a long, hard workday he would ask his son if this was the kind of work that he wanted to do for the rest of his life. He made sure that Moises Junior understood how low the pay was for all of this labor. His son learned the lesson well, and set his sights on the university and a teaching degree. Moises senior had done his own form of teaching, and he had done it very well.

Never afraid of hard work, Lupe wanted desperately to find a job to help support her children's educational expenses. She asked the city officials in Villa Garcia for any type of work, including sweeping streets. When these requests did not produce work, she learned to sew. This gave her the skills she needed to find work in the factories in several of the larger cities which surround Villa Garcia. Sometimes she travelled for over an hour to get to work.

Lupe knew that factory workers were often released in their mid 30's to bring in younger, more energetic workers, who were willing to work for lower wages. Seeing the handwriting on the wall, Lupe learned how to do multiple jobs in the factory, including how to lead others. These skills, coupled with her experience, kept her in high demand, even as many of her peers were losing their jobs.

Lupe taught her daughters to sew so that they would always have a trade to fall back on in case of emergencies. Yet, Lupe's real goal for her children was education. She says,

> "I always give my children moral support and inspiration. I can't always give them economic support, but I have confidence in them. But, sometimes kids appreciate things more when they have to work to help accomplish their goals."

Lupe reflected further,

> "I have been educated by my family. A good education begins in the home. We were taught right from wrong. I was taught to respect everyone. Like I tell my kids, one can be ignorant, but one can always respect other people, no matter how ignorant they are. Where there is respect, there is peace. If I treat you bad, you will treat me bad. So, yes, I have been educated in the moral sense."

In middle school, Mireya's favorite subject was agriculture. She helped her dad on the ranch by feeding the pigs, shearing the lambs, cleaning the corral, and watching the piglets. She would also help her dad in the fields, harvesting tomatoes, squash, peaches, and other fruit. As she got older and learned to sew, she helped her mom in the factory. The lessons that Mireya learned about hard work and low pay were the impetus for her to continue her education. Like her brother, Moises, she was taught a valuable lesson by her parents.

Recently, Mireya reflected on her last year in the university before completing her degree. She said,

"In my seventh semester in the university I took seven classes. Most of my classmates were women, and Dulce became a friend who took me under her wing. When I didn't see my family on weekends, she invited me to stay with her and her family. Her family is very nice and they have taken care of me. I was renting a room with another student during the week, but I didn't see her often. I worked during the day from 8 until 2, then I'd go home to shower and eat before heading to the university. My classes were from 4 until 9:30 p.m. On my free time I did homework and studied."

She continued,

"Sometimes I played basketball, jogged, or exercised. I also liked to read when there was time. And I have always loved to sing. Sometimes when I was cleaning I would sing songs of worship. I used to be in the church choir and I loved it. I miss that part of my life. But now, when I go to church, I sing loud and with plenty of joy. I also love to dance and have fun. Like the saying goes, there is a time for everything."

In talking about the future Mireya says,

"I have dreams now. The first one was recently completed, and I have finished my degree with the help of God. The next one is to start a child care center in Villa Garcia to help mothers who need to work or return to school. I also want to help Weavers of Hope in the same way that they have helped me. I want to help others in my community to achieve their goals. I know how it feels to have a dream and not be able to accomplish it for financial reasons. In my life I have gone through many obstacles and different experiences. I have learned from my mistakes and they have made me stronger. Through sacrifice and persistence, I now value what I have and I thank God that I have made it this far."

Mireya graduated from the university in the summer of 2010. She fulfilled her own dreams and those of her parents.

When you enter Lupe's home there are three university degrees framed and hanging on the wall. The place for the fourth one is waiting. In three years Lupita's degree will complete the set. No one has any doubts about that. The degrees constantly remind Lupe of her proudest achievements. Now, she has time to focus on her grandchildren.

Lupe is now a leader on the parent's committee for Weavers of Hope. She, along with the other parents on the committee, helps to set the vision for how we continue to grow and improve the program. She is a strong believer in the requirements that we place on the students regarding good grades, sponsor communications, community service, and ethical behavior. She says,

"We have had good growth on the parent's committee, but there is still a small group who are doing most of the work. We need to prepare the others and show them how they can help us."

Lupe goes on to say,

"We need more Mexicans and former students to support the work. I also want our parents to feel more responsible for all that we do. It feels good to support the organization, and to serve other people. It feels good to help. Sometimes people think that I get a salary from Weavers of Hope, and they say lots of things. But the truth is that no one makes me do this work. I do it because I like it, I believe in it, and I want to. I am thankful for all of the support."

Lupe concluded the interview with these comments,

"My children's education has made a positive impact on our family. Our kids feel stronger. Their degrees hang in our home as trophies of our sacrifices. They remind us of all of the work and hard times. Sometimes my girls were sad because they didn't have nice clothes. I would always tell them that some day it would change when they had secure, good jobs. I would tell them that after all of the hard work that we would overcome. I knew that I had to fight for my kids to have an education, and I hope that they will do the same for their children."

Lupe continues to be an outstanding community leader for Weavers of Hope. Her insights and visions, along with those of all of the other parents who are involved in this work, are critical to our continued success. These people, and their children, are the ones who will guide Weavers of Hope into the future.

*"May God bless you with enough foolishness to believe that you can make a difference in this world; So that you can do what others claim cannot be done."*

A Franciscan Benediction

# Julieta

It is 7 p.m. on a Saturday night in mid October with cool fall air and the anticipation of the impending explosion of colors on the trees. Another season of college football has started to unfold. The restaurant's dining room is filled with lively conversation about sports, travel, a wedding engagement, and a myriad of other pleasant topics. Soft music plays in the background, and each table is carefully adorned with fresh flowers and fine china. The harmony of the setting fills the air like a fine bouquet of flowers.

It is 7 p.m. on the same Saturday night in the kitchen of that same restaurant. Orders are shouted across a metal counter. *Dame la mesa dos*...give me the order for table two. The sounds of clanging pots, pans, dishes, and silverware flood through the hot, steamy kitchen. Four men hurriedly prepare meals over six open flames. Sweat forms on the brows of the staff as they work furiously to keep the clients in their festive mood. It is far from harmonious.

As in many restaurants and workplaces, there are two different worlds coexisting in the same establishment. The world of the clients is largely focused on an evening of relaxation, good conversation, and fine dining. It is easy, almost natural, to live in that world and be largely unaware of the chaos and stress that exists in the kitchen. Seldom do the clients get a glimpse of the other world. They often treat the wait staff with friendliness and courtesy, but their awareness usually ends there.

The kitchen staff, largely composed of immigrants, is very aware of the great chasm that separates them. Julieta is on the kitchen staff tonight. At other times, she crosses over into the world of those who are economically secure. She flashes back to being five years old by a swimming pool in Florida, and hearing strange, unfamiliar conversations. That was her earliest recollection that other languages existed.

Tonight, she ponders the vastness of the separation between the two groups as she goes in and out of the kitchen, bringing out the food. It is one of many formative experiences that have shaped the person she has become. She has never experienced poverty, nor has she lived on the margins of society, yet she is sensitive to the economic and cultural differences. Face to face, personal encounters have heightened her awareness and influenced her worldview.

Julieta has formed a friendship with Mateo, one of the immigrants. Over time and with building trust, he slowly revealed his story to her. As they shared a meal and talked, he wondered if she would withdraw when she heard of the harsh realities that have shaped him. She didn't. He decided to trust her with another chapter from his life, always unsure of where her breaking point would be.

Mateo was born in what is now the city of Nezahualcoyotl, Neza for short, on the outskirts of Mexico City. It emerged from a slum which was built on one of Mexico City's largest open-pit landfills. The disgusting smell and the huge dump were directly visible from the high school which Mateo's younger brother attended. During Mateo's childhood, Neza was without running water, sewers, paved streets, and public telephones. It was also extremely violent and dangerous.

Mateo, like many undocumented workers in the U.S., fled his home in search of work to help support his mother and six siblings. His family often looked to him as the best hope for supporting them. He began working when he was seven years old decorating candles for a small neighborhood business. At an early age, he demonstrated a determination and maturity well beyond his years. The family has always counted on him, and he has never disappointed them.

Julieta had noticed how fast and effectively he worked. He moved with a sense of determination and skill. Other members of the restaurant staff relied on him. Mateo cleared tables, ran food, and was in constant motion. He was different from most of the other staff. Even when doing the lesser jobs, he carried himself with a sense of dignity. He was respectful and polite to everyone, both customers and co-workers. While many of the other staff members complained and cursed, Mateo did his work quietly without any signs of agitation or profanity.

As the chapters of his life were revealed, Julieta would learn the story of his migration to the U.S. on foot via a harsh, life-taking desert in southern Arizona. The terrain that he walked is called "The Devil's Highway". Luis Alberto Urrea's book, with the same name, chronicles the story of 26 men who attempted to cross on this path in May of 2001. After walking for six days in the sweltering heat and wandering about 50 miles off course, 14 of the group died.

Julieta imagined the horrors of the desert, and felt compassion for Mateo and all of the others who made the crossing. Their level of desperation was beyond what she could comprehend. Yet, here was this young man, who had experienced a life-and-death ordeal, just working away in the restaurant without any signs of bitterness or resentment. Only a thankfulness to have work and a source for sending money home to his family.

Julieta learned that Mateo sewed his own clothes, cooked his meals, and studied English in every spare minute that he had. His work ethic and determination to succeed were obvious to anyone who got to know him. Although gentle and easy on the surface, there was a quiet intensity which burned inside Mateo. Julieta felt drawn to him.

Eventually, Julieta would learn that at least ten others on the staff of this restaurant had made the same journey. She wondered how many undocumented immigrants had lost their lives on The Devil's Highway.

Julieta was using her job in the restaurant to help to pay for her undergraduate degree in the university. She took courses that dealt with poverty, globalization, and immigration. In the classroom she gained a solid academic foundation for understanding many of the complex issues which surround these topics. But, it was easy to be mentally aware and emotionally distant.

The stories that she heard from Mateo and her co-workers transformed the academic concepts into vivid realities. Being with people who had endured this degree of human suffering transformed the hard facts into cutting, personal realities. It all became very alive and powerful for Julieta. She internalized the struggles of the poor and felt new levels of caring and compassion.

One morning before her classes, Julieta sat in a trendy coffee shop doing a reading assignment on migration and globalization for her Anthropology course. The text talked about rural farmers who could not compete with large agri-businesses in selling their crops. The open markets were forcing the peasant farmers out of their traditional means of survival. The result was a swarming to the mega-cities of Latin America in search of industrial jobs.

She took another bite of her scone as she read the story of a Zapotec Indian family in Oaxaca that migrated to Neza, outside of Mexico City. A chilling shock came over her as she remembered Mateo's story of his birth place. Suddenly, her scone did not taste so good.

Julieta reflected on how a person can come from such an impoverished background and still maintain their dignity and sense of hope. Working in the restaurant was good for her. It put her squarely in the middle of the two different worlds that exist. She realized how important it was to have personal relationships with people from different cultures, races, and economic backgrounds. A deep sense of being connected to all people permeated her soul. Julieta's developing value system embraced this core principle of unity.

Julieta grew up in a family that nurtured justice, equal rights, and an appreciation of the arts. They often discussed the social issues of the day. Her parents met at a crafts show in West Virginia, where her mother, Cher, was selling her sculptures and paintings. Cher is an accomplished folk artist.

Harry, Julieta's father, was at the show representing the local artisans whose hand-crafted quilts adorned the tables and booths. Harry's governmental job was to help the artisans find outlets for their products, thereby helping them to generate income and lift themselves out of dire poverty. Eventually, he would leave this work to run the family produce business that operated a packing house for tomatoes.

Cher and Harry had active social consciences, and were committed to putting their beliefs into action. At home they shared their values with their children. They talked with them about the horrors of slavery and the tragic injustices which led to the Civil War. History lessons in the children's classrooms were deepened by ethical discussions around the dinner table.

Julieta grew up learning about the discrimination that the American Indians faced. She was taught about political activism and speaking out. Her mom occasionally took her to demonstrations in favor of protecting the rights of the American Indians.

Yet, despite their advanced social consciences, both of her parents were sometimes distant and wrapped up in their own worlds. The folk art festivals and craft shows required Cher to be gone on many weekends. Harry's job in the family business was demanding. During these times, Julieta was often left to care for herself. She also sensed that it was her responsibility to help in raising her younger sister, Raven. A close bond developed between the two girls.

Gabriel, her older brother by five years, was often engaged with his own activities. Because of the age and gender differences, he was often left alone to fend for himself. This fostered a great deal of independence in him.

Gabriel was, and continues to be, an extremely creative person. As a young boy, he won multiple awards for his writing, including the prestigious Young Authors recognition.

Gabriel's creativity tended to isolate him from his peers growing up. From a young age he stood out as an individual. His mother fondly tells stories of his obsession with flying. For several years he wore a cape everywhere he went, including to school. No matter what people said he refused to believe that it was impossible for him to fly. Cher encouraged his fantasy, even defending the claims he made to classmates that he was able to fly.

Now, years later, Gabriel no longer wears a cape, but he continues to dream and live in a world of his own making. Like his mother, he found his passion in painting and creating. His paintings, which are often sold alongside his mother's, are filled with the same imagination that led him to believe he could fly as a little boy.

Gabriel was not the only creative, artistic child in the family. Julieta and Raven filled many hours together writing and performing plays that blended the realities of their daily lives with the vivid stirrings in their young imaginations.

Julieta's parents had always had a love for antiques, and had been collectors of various pieces for many years. It seemed then like a dream come true for Harry and Cher when they purchased a large, historic, federal-style home in Granville, Ohio, about 30 miles east of Columbus. The home, built in 1824, typified the architecture of the Federal Period in the early Republic. The house, like many of its period, reflected the early European immigrant desire to repeat and mirror the ascetic ideals of their homeland.

Julieta and the other children were soon caught up in the house project with their parents. It became somewhat of a hobby for all of them. They now had a perfect place for displaying the antique furniture that they had been collecting. Small tables and desks were frequently used. The use of wallpapers and textiles replaced wooden, paneled walls.

Before moving into the historic home, Harry was offered a Chief Operating Officer job with a large produce company and packing house in Columbus, Ohio. His considerable experience in the family produce company along with the many key contacts he had made gave him just the right skill set for the demanding, new job. He decided to take the job.

Upon arrival in Granville, Julieta and Raven were enrolled in an independent school where the curriculum was very different from the one used in the public school system. The classes were composed of no more than four students. They were not divided by a hierarchical grade or age system.

Each group was named after an important writer, artist, or philosopher. Julieta was placed in the Asimov group. Issac Asimov was considered one of the most prominent science fiction writers during his lifetime. The school curriculum included the self-directed study of art, poetry, and history.

Julieta fell in love with the small classes and the school's liberal arts focus. She felt safe and comfortable in her intimate, little study group. She had Raven close by, and life in the new home was pulling the family together in some good ways. She did not know that this home, which was loved so much by the entire family, would be the last they would ever share together as a family.

The dreams that were becoming a reality in the Granville home slowly came to an end in 1993 when her parents divorced after 20 years of marriage. The divorce was hard on the entire family, but the burden fell mainly on the children. After their father was awarded custody, the children moved to a suburb of Columbus and began a radically new life.

Julieta, for the first time in her life, entered the public school system. The alternative school had provided her with a wonderful liberal arts education, but they neglected many of the core classes that are required in the public schools. Embarrassingly, Julieta was put in sixth grade, two years behind her age group. This was a humiliating experience for her. She hated being isolated from her peer group, and resented every part of the school environment.

As she entered high school a couple of years later, her grades were poor and her attitude was worse. Harry was busy at work and involved in trying to make his new marriage a success. Julieta didn't have a curfew. She managed to make mediocre grades with little or no studying. She often felt off balance and depressed.

Her stepmother was diagnosed with manic-depressive, bi-polar disorder during Julieta's sophomore year in high school. She left the family as Julieta began her senior year. Harry suddenly had more time on his hands, and began to pay more attention to the troubling signs exhibited by Julieta. They began to reconnect on a deeper level.

However, the real turning point for Julieta was the interest of a geology teacher. She saw real potential in Julieta, a good brain, and a young lady who could blossom with a little work. She encouraged her to do her homework, to read the book, and to participate in class. One day, she gave her an opportunity to orally respond to a question in class. As her peers snickered, thinking that Julieta had no idea of how to answer the question, she stunned all of them. She let loose with a complete, logical, and fully accurate answer to the question. She was on her way back to academic excellence. Her grade point average soared to 3.5 in her senior year. She was transformed.

Julieta was accepted at Kent State University, near Cleveland, Ohio. She began her university career right where she left off in high school, working hard, and making the dean's list. However, she lost focus after the first year in the university, flunking out of school in her third semester.

After taking a year off to re-evaluate her life, she came out with a new attitude, ready to work and to finish her university degree. She had the clarity of vision to realize that she had already succeeded academically, both in high school and in her freshman year at the university. She was confident that she could build on those prior achievements and take them to new levels. And this time, she was determined to transform the course of her life.

Julieta enrolled in Columbus State Community College. She applied herself in her studies and was soon back on the dean's list. She read a variety of influential books, and thought considerably about the direction she wanted her life to take. The philosophy of empowering yourself and speaking truth to power were concepts that made sense to her. Julieta was convinced that the best way to empower herself was with education. She dove into her academic work with dedication and tenacity. In two years, she received her associate's degree in liberal arts with top grades.

There was no doubt in Julieta's mind that this was only the beginning for her. She was accepted into the art conservation program at the University of Delaware. On her first visit to the campus she fell in love with it, knowing that this was where she wanted to be. The next phase of her education would bring even greater achievements and changes.

Julieta needed to work in order to help finance her education. She decided to work in the restaurant where she met Mateo and learned about the life of desperate Latin American citizens who became undocumented immigrants in the U.S. By working there, she would have a way to help pay for her education. Juggling a job and classes would be tough, but she was focused and ready to make it work.

While at the university, Julieta learned of study abroad opportunities where she could earn college credits in Spanish while immersing herself in new cultures and customs. Excited by these opportunities, she pored over the details of the various programs and locations, finally settling on the University of Granada in Spain. This was the first of several international learning programs that she would experience.

This way of learning was fantastic for Julieta. The non-traditional school of her earlier years had prepared her to be open and excited by creative learning experiences. She hungered for more of these opportunities. As she researched the wide variety of study abroad opportunities, her mind raced with excitement and curiosity.

The following year, she decided to spend a full semester at a university in Puebla, Mexico, 80 miles southeast of Mexico City. This experience would support her choice of a minor in Latin American studies. It would also give her a chance to go deeper into the lives, customs, and culture of these people.

Julieta took classes in literature, history, and geography, all of them taught in Spanish. The cultural and academic cornucopia of learning was totally captivating and stimulating for her. Her mind rapidly processed the experiences, and looked for more. The faster they came at her, the more she wanted, both in depth and variety.

In the middle of all of this time of fertile growth, Julieta began to notice an underlying reality that was deeply disturbing for her. At first the university in Puebla seemed much like any prosperous North American university. Peacocks roamed freely over the carefully manicured lawns and gardens. The students generally came from affluent families, and were often accompanied by bodyguards. Seeing students with nice clothes, cars, and extra money for discretionary spending was much like what she saw in the U.S.

However, a great difference occurred when she left campus and was swallowed by neighborhoods of rampant poverty. The contrasts that existed when she crossed the campus border were jolting. She thought back to the scenes in the Doctor Zhivago movie where the opulence of the lavish, Russian banquet was surrounded by the poverty of the peasants in the street. This realization hit her hard. It would be a life lesson that she would carry with her.

The following summer saw Julieta move deeper into experiences of injustice and inequality. She accepted a job as a research assistant on Isla Colon, an island in the Panamanian archipelago. The archipelago is comprised of 9 islands, 52 keys, and over 200 islets.

A century ago, American banana companies built on several of the islands and hired Afro-Caribbean workers to supplement the indigenous workforce. When the companies abandoned the plantations, they left behind a dramatically altered culture, one that would eventually evolve into an eco-tourism bonanza for the realtors. It is beginning to compete with some of the longer established countries in eco-tourism, like Costa Rica and Belize.

The documentary and research project that Julieta worked on, examined the effects of the tourist culture on the lives of the indigenous island dwellers. Working under an established applied anthropologist, Julieta saw and experienced the poverty on the island. Her job involved conducting extensive interviews with the foreign travelers. She fit in easily with them in appearance, education, and social skills. They felt comfortable talking with her, and the information that she gathered was a key piece in the filming of the documentary. Each day saw her crossing back and forth between the people on both sides of the economic divide, much like in the restaurant's kitchen. The contrasts in wealth that she had seen earlier in Puebla, Mexico were even greater here.

Foreign-owned, luxury hotels with gourmet food and pampered guests were surrounded by people living in shacks with no water or electricity. Often, the hotels forced the people out of their homes in acquiring choice real estate for rock bottom prices. It was thinly veiled exploitation which made one wonder about the limits of human greed.

The local Panamanians were then hired to work in the hotels for salaries which were so low that it was its own form of slavery. The lust for massive profits trumped any sense of decency and fairness. Julieta observed all of this, processing it during conversations with her co-workers which went well into the nights. She was outraged at the level of injustice.

On Sunday mornings the island people would don the finest of their clothing to attend church services. As they walked to their modest churches they passed lithe, tanned bodies in the skimpiest of bikinis. Their community had become a playground. Their cultural standards of decency were being trampled on by the encroaching tourist population.

The tourism was also having an environmental impact on the islands. The lights from the hotels were distracting baby sea turtles, and many turned up dead as they were never able to find their way to the water after hatching.

Racist comments and mockery about the simplicity of the native's life style were sometimes heard from groups of tourists. Julieta was deeply saddened by the lack of respect that she saw. Angry tears welled up inside of her as she vowed to dedicate herself to living in solidarity with the poor. She yearned to be their voice and to help them in whatever ways that she could. This would be her life's mission.

Before graduating with her bachelor's degree from the University of Delaware, Julieta had one more opportunity to hone her international awareness. It was on the continent of Africa, in Nairobi, the capital and largest city in Kenya. With approximately three million residents, it is the most populous city in East Africa. It is also one of the most prominent cities in Africa, both politically and financially.

Nairobi terrified Julieta. Throughout the 1990s Nairobi struggled with rising crime and earned the dubious nickname of "Nairobbery". In 2001 it was listed as one of the most insecure cities in the world, with nearly one third of the residents experiencing a robbery. A high percentage of the armed robberies and carjackings were violent. Many attributed this high level of crime to police corruption, which allowed the perpetrators to go unpunished.

Julieta found herself in the midst of this unrest as a part of her work in helping to staff the World Social Forum. The annual forum includes organizations, world-wide, who are working for positive social change. Julieta was working the help desk and assisting with translation among the English and Spanish speaking attendees.

This was the greatest level of poverty and danger that Julieta had seen in any of her international experiences. Riots broke out around the forum as the residents fought to obtain the low paying volunteer jobs associated with the conference. Glue-sniffing street kids, high on a variety of drugs, attacked the food tents ready to fight for whatever they could steal. The police protection was lacking, and Julieta lived and worked in constant fear. It was a place where she would never want to return.

Upon graduation from the University of Delaware, Julieta was accepted into the masters program at the School for International Training Graduate Institute in Brattleboro, Vermont. She wanted to dedicate her life to working on solutions to the problems and injustices which she had personally seen over the last several years. She wanted to make a difference in the world, and she was empowering herself to do it with a greater level of education. Her master's degree would be in Sustainable Development and would focus on long-term solutions.

Before beginning the program she spent the summer after completing her undergraduate degree on yet another continent, Asia. As part of a grant that the Department of International Studies received, she went to Seoul, South Korea. The grant was to study consumption patterns in South Korea. Once again she found herself conducting interviews with citizens from all economic classes, and compiling data about spending trends.

As Julieta began her master's program, she entered into that phase of her education with an unusually diverse resume of experiences, an excellent academic record, and a passion to make a difference in people's lives. It was a powerful background to frame her studies.

As Julieta neared the completion of her master's degree, there was a requirement for a 6-12 month internship in the field. I met Julieta when she submitted an application to work for Weavers of Hope. As I read her resume, I remember being a bit overwhelmed at the extent and diversity of her international experiences. How could one so young have done so much?

In the phone interview, I knew instinctively that she was the right person for Weavers of Hope. She told me that she was a little nervous about the interview, and I admired her honesty and candor in admitting it. However, just to make sure, I arranged to meet her in Brattleboro, Vermont. I was in Massachusetts visiting family, so the trip to Brattleboro was only a half day drive. We talked, walked, and got to know each other. There was no doubt that she was the person we dreamed of finding. In September of 2008, Julieta became the first paid employee of Weavers of Hope.

It took little time to see how motivated, intelligent, responsible, and creative Julieta was. She hit the ground running and we quickly gave her more responsibilities. The job included translating student and sponsor letters, helping in grant preparation and documentation of the results, preparing and running large parts of the monthly student meetings, working with the parents committee, and interviewing potential candidates for entry into the program. She worked beautifully with Fran and the people of Villa Garcia.

When I first visited Villa Garcia a few months after Julieta joined us, what I observed brought tears of joy to my eyes. To see how she was accepted and embraced by Fran, the parents, and the students was beyond my wildest dreams, and I do dream wildly. So it has been with Julieta for over two years now. She has become so vital to our success. She has also become a part of our family. I hope and pray for the funding that will allow us to pay her more generously in the years ahead.

While working for Weavers of Hope, Julieta wrote her Capstone Report (similar to a thesis) on sustainable scholarships as they relate to the work of Weavers of Hope. In it she identified some interesting insights which will shape our program as we go into the future.

She recognized the importance of focusing on preserving cultural and familial respect as first-generation university graduates complete their studies. The 20 plus university graduates from Weavers of Hope have received considerably more formal education than almost all of their parents. This leads to changes in values regarding jobs and life style. It offers the potential for a breakdown in family communications and less respect for cultural traditions. Julieta cautions that we must work hard to never let this happen.

In 2009, Julieta completed her oral examinations and received her master's degree. She has reconnected with Mateo in Mexico, and the two of them are talking of marriage and family. Julieta continues on with Weavers of Hope as a valued employee and friend.

> *"We can never see the end results, but that is
> the difference between the master builder and the worker.
> We are workers, not master builders, ministers, not messiahs.
> We are prophets of a future not our own."*
>
> Oscar Romero

# The Ripple Effect

Did you ever toss a rock into a pond of perfectly still water? As a boy, I was always fascinated by the ripples which spread out in concentric circles from the point of contact. It was mesmerizing to watch them travel out to distances beyond what seemed possible. When they would finally play out and the water would return to complete stillness, I would throw another stone into the middle of the pond and wait in anticipation for the next group of circles.

As an adult, I am still enraptured by the ripple effect in life. Actions, be they good, bad, or neutral, set into motion a whole series of events. The events are often unpredictable, but you know that they will come in some fashion. When they are not recognizable, you get the sense that they are occurring below the surface, on another level.

Yet, so many of my actions are done instinctively and without much thought as to what they might cause. It's hard for me to pay attention to vague, future possibilities when there is so much to be done. Much of life seems to focus on the point of impact, oblivious to the impending ripples which will follow.

Not surprisingly, the initial work of the Weavers of Hope sponsorship program has caused some very good ripples. Most of them were totally unforeseen when we began the project. However, in looking back, it is clear that they were part of the aftershocks.

On our early visits to Villa Garcia, as we passed through weathered doors and old buildings, we often found antique floor looms holding weavings in various states of completion. Rolls of brightly colored yarn surrounding the looms were like vibrant rainbows lighting up the otherwise drab areas. In the congested living areas, precious space was set aside for the hand-crafted looms. They seemed to be everywhere…in homes, garages, workshops, and courtyards.

When we asked questions about their use, it stirred up lively conversations that were bursting with energy and emotion. There was often a sadness, as when one speaks of a deceased loved one. Weaving was more than a job for most villagers. It was a creative experience, an art form, and a way of life. Their craft provided income and a livelihood. The eyes of the villagers glazed over into dream-like states as they spun the tales of times past.

The weaving tradition in Villa Garcia had been passed down from parents to children over many generations. Frequently, it was almost a ritualistic rite of passage into adulthood for the young apprentice. It was painful for the artisans to watch this way of life slowly erode over the years. Many of the weavers hung on to their dreams for a better tomorrow.

The weaving tales sometimes began with the search for the wool and dyes. The creation of the dyes in various parts of Mexico was an almost magical process. In certain parts of the country, the artisans drove winding, mountain roads into the high meadowlands to secure flowers, herbs, moss, and wood which would go into the dye kettle along with other secret ingredients. They guarded their secrets, like a chef with an award winning recipe. The indigenous weavers, along with many others, treated the entire process as a sacred ritual. They were meticulously respectful to take only what they needed from the land.

Mite-sized insects from the Nopal cactus are used to create a rich and varied array of red dyes. They are so highly valued that they have come to be called "red gold". It is from these intense, vibrant colors that the wool is dyed and the tapestries are woven. The parents had always envisioned leaving this legacy of artistry to their children and grandchildren.

In the 1970s there were truckloads of weavings being sent regularly from the village of Villa Garcia to various markets along both sides of the U.S./Mexico border. Over the years, the markets gave way to the pressures of cheaper labor in countries like China and the Philippines. Weavers were forced to go to work in the factories in order to survive. Their dreams of passing this art form on to their children were disappearing.

As the conversations unfolded between our bands of travelers and the residents of Villa Garcia, we wondered if there was some way for us to enter into the weaving struggle with them. We felt drawn to the strong emotional connection between the weavers and their craft.

It seemed as though we had uncovered a precious, hidden gem in their workmanship. The locally produced tapestries sang of quality, from the tight weaving techniques to the vibrant colors and designs. The prices, by U.S. standards, were shockingly inexpensive. It was from these conversations with the villagers that a new Weavers of Hope project began to emerge.

Most of the visitors from the U.S. were familiar with the concepts of fair trade coffee and chocolate. Many faith communities of various denominations are actively involved in bringing these products to their congregations. A growing number of concerned citizens are also embracing fair trade products.

When the visitors to Villa Garcia began to hear the stories about the loss of a way of life, their hearts were touched. They were immediately sympathetic to the plight of the workers, and open to searching out ways to help them to maintain the long-standing tradition of weaving.

The group from Austin began to think of ways to extend the concepts of fair trade to include the weavings that the artisans of Villa Garcia were producing. Besides helping individuals, we all dreamed of having a small part in helping to preserve a cornerstone of their art and culture. That was the hope, and it has worked. Unfortunately, it has only worked to a limited extent so far. At this time we work with only one family business. However, the potential exists for significant, future growth.

In the family we work with, the father trained his sons on the various aspects of his craft. In the past, when sufficient markets existed, cousins and spouses have helped in the business. In current times, with shrinking markets, they are struggling to make a living.

We began by asking Lupe, the spokesman for the family business, if we could explore some possibilities with him. Lupe is a large, gentle man with a soft smile and a serious attitude. He has youthful skin, unlike many of the outdoor workers, and eyes which sparkle brightly. He is also quiet and reserved by nature. As he mostly listened and observed, you got the idea that his mind was functioning at a high level, with clarity and perception.

At this point we were unproven strangers in the village who had purchased a few rugs from him. Trust develops slowly in many cultures, and we would learn that it would take time to establish a trusting relationship with Lupe. I have enjoyed watching this relationship continue to grow over the years.

We asked Lupe for his thoughts on what he would consider to be a fair price to pay for the weavings which his family were producing. This direct question seemed to cause him great consternation. He hemmed and hawed, rubbed his chin, and pondered the question for what seemed like an eternity. Finally, he gave us a price that seemed to be on the low side.

Eventually, we agreed to start with that price. Several months later, we voluntarily increased what we were paying Lupe. The tapestries which we were receiving were of a consistently high quality. Our intention was to pay the artists a just wage. We wanted this family to continue their craft, maintain a sense of dignity, and be able to provide the necessities of life for themselves and their children.

Over the years we have continued to increase what we pay them. The price of the wool and dyes has risen, as has the cost of groceries. In a small way, we are helping to sustain this family. We are in the struggle with them to keep the weaving tradition alive.

The double bonanza from this work, that is equally beautiful, is that all of the profits from the sales of these rugs are plowed back into the student sponsorship program. This gives us additional funding to help more young people in Villa Garcia to continue their education. Both the weavers and the students are benefitting.

As Lupe has watched this unfold, I have seen his trust in us growing. Weavers of Hope included one of Lupe's nieces in its sponsorship program. He could directly see that we were keeping our promises. I could almost feel him smiling on the inside and being pleased that we were true to our word.

We have also learned that Lupe is a man of his word, and that we can trust him. A hand shake is our contract, and it is a contract that has never been broken on either side.

The fair trade weaving project was the first clearly identifiable ripple that came out of our initial work in the village. There would be more.

Stepping back to another place and time…in 1831, Frederic Ozanam enrolled in the School of Law at the Sorbonne, University of Paris. He was instrumental in reviving a student organization which had been suspended during the French Revolution of 1830. The group discussed a wide variety of social topics. Because of the politically charged environment following the revolution they consciously excluded politics from their discussions.

Challenged by a fellow student, Frederic and five associates founded an offshoot organization a couple of years later to assist the poor. "The Society of Saint Vincent de Paul" (SVDP) was named in honor of their patron, who lived from 1581 to 1660. He was called "The Father of the Poor".

Frederic was a husband, father, professor, and servant of the poor. He was one of the first to write extensively on the issues of social justice. The Society was first established in 1845 in the U.S. in the city of St. Louis. Today there are almost a million members in 130 countries who are actively working in this organization.

The Society of SVDP offers tangible assistance to those in need on a person to person basis. This aid may take the form of intervention or consultation, or through direct dollar or in-kind service. The help is provided while consciously maintaining the confidentiality and dignity of those who are served. The Society also recognizes that it must assume a role of advocacy for those who are defenseless or voiceless. Some 12 million people are helped annually in the U.S.

After Weavers of Hope began the educational sponsorship program in 2003, Fran began to make trips to Austin to speak to various groups about the work. Some of the groups that she spoke with included members who belonged to local Society of Saint Vincent de Paul groups. These local groups, which exist around the globe, are called conferences. There were also several members of the founding team for Weavers of Hope who were active in the work of SVDP. Thus began another part of the ripple effect in Villa Garcia.

SVDP has a "twinning" concept. Conferences with more financial resources are encouraged to partner with poorer conferences, which are often located in developing nations. This international sharing allows the outreach to the poor to grow to more impoverished areas around the world.

Three SVDP conferences in the Austin, Texas area had met Fran and were impressed with her personally, along with the work that she was doing. In some instances it had been difficult for the Austin conferences to get regular status reports from the conferences that they were helping in developing nations. The Austin SVDP groups felt like the poorer conferences were using the financial aid in positive ways, but without the communications, there was a lingering doubt. After meeting Fran, they were comfortable in recommending that Villa Garcia become a twinning location.

This inspired Fran to find various people in her community who were excited about the work of SVDP. Together, they worked with the pastor in Villa

Garcia and the bishop in Aguascalientes to begin a local SVDP conference.

Fran was teaching the people about empowerment, setting goals, and action. She also helped them past a major hurdle - being able to communicate with the clergy. Many of the villagers had previously put church leaders on pedestals in their minds, feeling unworthy to talk with them as fellow human beings. This work came to fruition with the formation of a local SVDP conference in Villa Garcia. It began in October 2003.

The conferences in Austin have been providing assistance to the Villa Garcia conference ever since. The twinning concept is successful and flourishing.

The people of the SVDP conference in Villa Garcia meet weekly for prayer, fellowship, and a concern for their neighbors who have even less than they do. Specific cases are reviewed, and assistance is provided in the village and in various surrounding, rural communities. It is a situation of the poor helping the poor. The Villa Garcia group publishes detailed, monthly status reports to the SVDP conferences in Austin. The trust is solid on both sides.

The members of the SVDP conference in Villa Garcia collect clothes, food, household items, books, and hygiene items. These are loaded up into Fran's truck and brought to the rural areas. Personal relationships of love, respect, friendship, prayer, and sharing have developed. It goes well beyond economics. The holistic outreach from neighbor to neighbor touches body, mind, and spirit.

Often, Fran encounters excellent students in the rural areas who cannot afford to continue in school. She encourages them to apply for the Weavers of Hope educational sponsorship program. Several of them are now in our program, and succeeding in school at levels beyond what anyone thought was possible. The outward ripples of the SVDP work have found their way back to the source…education.

When Fran first told me that she was in the process of building a large hospitality and retreat center, I thought she was crazy. How could an older, single lady coordinate a project of such magnitude? Where would she find the funds to complete such a project? When I learned that there was no water source to the building, the project became even more daunting in my mind.

Fran's dream of completing the construction, her faith in God, and her belief in herself triumphed over those difficulties. She wanted this center for the people of Mexico, and she wanted it to be named in honor of her deceased father. She was convinced that it would happen, and she was right on target. This project, along with many others, has taught me so much. I have learned to believe in things that are bigger than what I can comprehend.

Kiko led the initial stages of construction, doing much of the work himself and supervising the work of some local men who were desperately in need of jobs. It was gratifying to see local laborers focus on the construction with such love and attention to detail. They were thankful for meaningful work and an income. For their families, it was life sustaining. Little by little, we all watched the building progress, still wondering about the water. Fran's faith remained steadfast.

As Fran and the work of Weavers of Hope became better known in the Austin area, there were a number of men who were touched by the stories of the people in Villa Garcia. They wanted to help, and the construction project provided the opportunity. Many of them were retired from a variety of careers, yet still healthy and vibrant. Plus, they had caring hearts. They were experienced in electrical work, plumbing, water systems, carpentry, and a variety of other skills that were needed for Casa Clemens.

Teams of men formed groups to do specific parts of the construction. They talked with family members and friends about the project. As the stories spread, many others wanted to help. Financial aid came from a variety of sources. This allowed the groups to purchase the supplies that were needed for the work.

The first group of men with carpentry skills drove south to Villa Garcia. They built the furniture for the bedrooms and left behind a blueprint that other local workers could follow. Bed frames, night tables, and bookcases were designed and constructed.

Shortly after that, a team of electricians went to the village to install all of the wiring, light fixtures, wall sockets, and switches. They teamed with locals, and worked side by side despite the language barriers. Before they left, Casa Clemens lit up the night skies, like a glowing city on a mountain. Let there be light.

About a year later, another group of men went to install all of the plumbing, including a cistern to catch rain water. They set up a purification system for the drinking water. Clean drinking water and flush toilets were somewhat of an anomaly for the area. Shortly after that, Fran and Kiko would work out an agreement with the city of Villa Garcia to provide city water to Casa Clemens.

Things were steadily moving along. One by one, my doubts about the project were dropping away. Fran was more matter-of-fact, always sure that Casa Clemens would happen in God's time. Her dream of a hospitality and retreat center, named after her father, was becoming a reality.

In 2008, Casa Clemens opened to the public, hosting the monthly meeting for all of the Weavers of Hope scholarship students and their families. Food, fellowship, and laughter filled the rooms. It was the joyous completion of an eight-year project.

The large, rectangular-shaped meeting space stretched along the west side of Casa Clemens. It could easily hold several hundred people. Natural light poured in from the windows, glass paneled doors, and skylights. It made the space cheerful and welcoming. Potted plants, reveling in the sunlight, added another dimension of warmth to the room. The pictures on the east wall told the stories of relationships. Fran's family, the people of Mexico, and her Weavers of Hope family told of a life well-lived and abundant in joy and happiness. Fran lives with meager material possessions, but she is rich in all the things that matter.

On the corner, at one end of the meeting room is the chapel. Abundant light flows in from the windows which look out onto the rolling hills of the countryside. Locally woven rugs add warmth and texture to the floors. The icons and pictures provide a comforting, spiritual ambiance. It is unlike the lavish, ornate cathedrals, but it rings true to a savior born in a stable among the peasant farmers of that time.

The hosting of the initial retreat marked the spiritual birth of the facility. The first Mass was celebrated in the chapel. University graduates from the Weavers of Hope sponsorship program gave talks and witnesses. They were the living fruition of our dreams. Many of them continue to speak inspirationally at both retreats and monthly student meetings.

Next to the chapel is a large, fully functional kitchen. It has all the comforts of home with refrigerator, microwave oven, and stove. The folding tables are pushed together to allow for ample seating for a large group. It gives us a place to gather and share meals. We now had a home in Mexico.

The ten bedrooms are off the main hallway on the opposite side of the building, with large bathrooms at each end of the hall. Groups visiting Villa Garcia now had a place to stay with enough bedrooms for each traveler to have their own room. As I looked at the furniture, I remembered that first carpentry trip when the initial bed frames and night tables were built. There was a sense of history and connectedness. It felt good deep inside.

My favorite room is the library. It is in the center of the building, a cozy place to snuggle into on a cold day. Locally woven rugs, wall hangings, bookcases, comfortable sofas and chairs envelope me, like a hug from a loving grandmother.

The library is my sanctuary for prayer and meditation in the morning. I love to go there early, before anyone else is up, with a cup of coffee, a candle, and some incense burning. It feels like sacred space, safe and secure. In the evenings, it is a comfortable place for quiet and reading.

In the summer of 2010, Casa Clemens was the site of a two-week intensive English workshop. The classes met for five hours per day. They allowed students, teachers, and parents to take their English proficiency to new levels. Skits, music, cultural presentations, and dance were used to teach the traditional components of reading, writing, grammar, conversation, and listening. We laughed and learned together. Relationships deepened during those two weeks. Fran continues to find new uses for the building.

In 2009, it became clear to Fran that there was a need for a caretaker for Casa Clemens. Hosting all of the events, cooking, cleaning, and scheduling was too much for one person to do. Almost miraculously, that person emerged, right on cue. In the village of Copetillo, about two miles down the road from Casa Clemens, Martha was living in a crowded, small space with her parents and seven siblings. Martha is a loving, sincere, hard-working religious sister. She was looking for work and another place to live. Fran's immediate gut instinct, in that first conversation, was that Martha was the perfect person for the job. The caretaker role was filled.

Martha's presence as the guardian of Casa Clemens adds another dimension of welcoming to the center. Her love for plants and flowers has added a beautiful touch of warmth to Casa Clemens. The rugged desert landscape is now broken by the colorful flowers that adorn the entrance to Casa Clemens.

Martha carefully collects the eggs from the chickens in the mornings and prepares home-cooked omelets and fresh fruit for breakfast. She seems such a part of Casa Clemens, always bustling around, working, and smiling. She makes you feel good to be in her presence.

Casa Clemens stands tall, a monument to Fran's faith, work and determination. Her dad would be proud.

In the early years of Weavers of Hope, travel to Villa Garcia was done almost exclusively by the founding members of the organization. This was natural for a beginning organization.

Those were wonderful opportunities for bonding among us as we drove the 15 hours to Villa Garcia. The time in the car without distractions allowed us to have deep, meaningful conversations. It also allowed us to eat, sightsee, and laugh together. The fact that we were all so committed to the work gave us a common cause and a solid foundation to build from. I loved those trips.

One of the ladies who most often made the trips with me was Kay. To know Kay is to never forget her. She is plain spoken, direct, funny, and has a large, compassionate heart. She is also a firm believer in personal responsibilities. She will give you all that she has, but if you don't do your part…watch out!

Kay and I were members of a Saint Vincent de Paul conference in northwest Austin when we first met. I'll never forget my initial introduction to Kay. She was discussing one of the cases where SVDP provides assistance to needy families.

Kay had visited this particular family to interview them and provide help with their electricity bill, which was significantly in arrears. Austin summers are brutally hot, with temperatures often exceeding 100 degrees Fahrenheit. Utility bills are high.

It was the height of summer when Kay walked into this home. It was cold inside. She bluntly told the lady that it was no wonder that she needed help with electricity bills. Somehow, Kay was able to tell it like it is while still maintaining a touch of humor. People liked her.

Without calling the lady's house a meat locker, Kay did get the point across that people have to learn to live at much warmer temperatures in summer's punishing heat. Kay told her that no one can afford electricity when the thermostat is set so low. No dancing around the issue for Kay. She just laid it out there, plainly and directly. The lady received assistance, but only after hearing Kay's thoughts on the subject.

I was laughing to myself at her straight out approach. I had sometimes had the identical thoughts when doing SVDP case work, but was too timid to say anything. Now I had a model to follow. Even with my non-confrontational style, I later found myself in the home of another family we were trying to help. And there I was, telling these folks straight out that they needed to turn up their thermostat settings in the summer. That was the first of many lessons I learned from Kay.

On the trips to Villa Garcia, Kay would always have two large suitcases filled with used clothes, toys, and various household items. She had a whole network of family members and friends who saved things for her to take to Mexico. Kay would roll her eyes, and talk about how good the things were that were being discarded. I got the sense that she believed in using things thoroughly before buying replacements.

Nevertheless, the hand-me-downs were greatly appreciated in Villa Garcia. One person's discards are another person's treasure. The people of Villa Garcia always loved it when Kay would show up with her suitcases. The items that she brought were focused on what she knew the people most needed. It was like she directed her beneficiaries to not only give, but to give in a way that would provide the most help for the families in Mexico.

There were always little treats for the kids. Candy, small toys, school supplies, socks, and a variety of other things accompanied whatever the parents received. Often, we could not make it all the way to Villa Garcia before Kay's love and generosity for the people of Mexico burst forth.

We'd be driving through some remote little community with ramshackle houses and a multitude of kids playing outside, when Kay would ask me if we could stop. I always said yes. Then, in the middle of the country, in this poor little community, we'd pull over. Out would come the toys, candy, and some clothes. That was always one of my favorite parts of our trips south. The spontaneous joy that Kay generated was glorious to watch.

Kay knew more people in the Villa Garcia area than any of us. She would want to visit everyone, especially those with the least in terms of material things. She would listen to their stories, spend time with them, and walk away with a new set of friends. The kids followed her like the pied piper as the endless flow of candy and gum came out of her backpack.

Once, Kay decided that we needed to emphasize spirituality in a more direct way in Villa Garcia. She purchased Bibles in Spanish which were distributed at a monthly student meeting. The kids were thrilled to get the Bibles. Most of them had never owned a book before. The gift came with a lecture about the importance of living good lives and being a positive impact in their families and community. There was never a lost opportunity with Kay.

I have never met anyone who sincerely loved the Mexican people more than Kay. I would later learn that she had taught English as a second language (ESL) in Austin for over 20 years. Her network of Latin American friends in Austin was huge. She would become involved in their lives, way beyond a normal teacher/student relationship. She helped them with specific problems, provided guidance, attended quinceaneras and weddings, and was accepted like family.

Over the years since we began Weavers of Hope, there have been over 40 people who have visited Villa Garcia with us. As the stories were told, more and more people wanted to meet these simple, humble, Mexican people. They wanted to experience the work firsthand. There seemed to be a need in many of the travelers for a personal connection with people who live very different lives than what most of us have experienced. The warm, welcoming culture of the Mexican people and the open hearts of the visitors have forged many new relationships.

At first, bringing visitors to Villa Garcia was largely spontaneous. With prayer, time, and study, we have learned that these trips can be life changing for the visitors. The casual nature of the trips has gradually become more respectful of what is possible. Personal relationships with people who live in poverty teach powerful lessons. The respect for nurturing a holistic, cultural, and spiritual experience is now foundational in these trips.

The overall atmosphere continues to be gentle and laid back, but there is an underlying awareness that something much deeper is possible. It has the potential to be sacred time. From that growth, a trip like this is now called a Mission Awareness Trip. It is another ripple effect from the work of Weavers of Hope in Mexico.

Short-term mission experiences provide opportunities for travelers to experience other people in ways that never would happen if we stayed home. Our experiences outside of our comfort zone, with God's people in other cultures, or with people who struggle to survive, strengthen and transform us. This provides us with an opportunity to think, reflect, and change.

We are open to receiving from those we are called to serve, to learning, and to the risk of stretching ourselves. But, most of all, we are open to transformation. It is more about sharing who we are than what we do. It is about being, rather than doing. It is about communicating our love and concern across language barriers and cultural differences.

Transformation comes about when something inside us shifts, and despite ourselves, we find that we are no longer the person we used to be. It comes when we are open and present to the realities of other people's lives. Transformation requires prayer, reflection, and integration. It leads us to solidarity with those who are struggling.

Sometimes we find ourselves wanting to advocate on behalf of those we meet on the mission trip, and on the issues which affect their lives. Solidarity impacts our lifestyle. It leads us to new ways of living.

These are the things that we talk about in our pre-trip meetings. Sometimes, potential visitors are a little uncomfortable without having a list of things to accomplish. Many visitors have been on prior mission trips where there was "real" work to do. The idea of "hanging out" and getting to know the people caused them some mental discomfort. But, that is how relationships of trust are built. The trust is what makes our projects work so well.

As the years rolled by, other factors began to open the door for new travelers to be interested in visiting Villa Garcia on a Mission Awareness Trip. The talks that Fran gave in Austin allowed her to meet many people, some of whom expressed an interest in going to Mexico. Several of our Weavers of Hope volunteers spoke about the work both informally and formally to a variety of individuals and groups. More curiosity and interest arose. Another ripple has been in the transformation of minds and hearts.

On a football team, there needs to be a considerable amount of respect and mutual admiration between the quarterback and the offensive linemen. Without the linemen doing their jobs and blocking the opposing players, the quarterback will never have a chance to throw the long, touchdown pass to win the game. They need to work together to succeed.

I like to think of charitable work as the offensive linemen, and justice work as the quarterback. Both are necessary for unity, wholeness, and success. In our personal lives, some of us are linemen and some quarterbacks. We need those who are charitable to keep desperate people alive and hopeful while those who work for just social structures lobby for long-term changes. Together, the people who work on both fronts are vital in the quest for human rights.

Charity focuses on the needs of individuals or groups. It meets an immediate need which is often the symptom of a social problem. Justice invites us to analyze social situations or social structures, and to work for long-term solutions. It addresses the root causes of social issues which lead to individual problems.

In the case of homeless people, charity would invite us to work with the homeless community for shelter, food, jobs, and other forms of emergency assistance. Justice would have us looking into low-income housing projects, increased wages for the jobs on the economic bottom, tenants' rights, and enforcing building codes.

Weavers of Hope has both linemen and quarterbacks. Our primary mission is about empowering students to change their lives through education. This mission leans toward mostly long-term solutions. We envision university graduates finding meaningful work, supporting themselves, helping their families, and becoming community leaders. Their education will put them in a position to challenge unjust social structures in Mexican government and business. This latter goal is beyond the Weavers of Hope mission. Our goal is to help empower our graduates to take on these huge challenges.

Sometimes, our students need food, shoes, and transportation expenses to get them into a position to succeed in the classroom. These short term needs highlight the necessity of charity to go along with the longer term work of education. Our organization recognizes both needs.

Occasionally, Weavers of Hope receives special donations to be used for charitable causes. One such incident happened a few years ago and resulted in the $900 project, as I like to call it. We thought and prayed about how best to use the money. In the end, we decided to ask two of our most trusted adults from the local community to run the project. They took their work seriously.

Interviews, home visits, conversations with trusted family members and friends, and prayer led them to discern where to use the money. At the end of the project they presented a booklet that was worthy of a college level report. It contained photos of the people being helped, a write-up on the particular situation, how much money was given, and how the money would be used. All of us were so proud of the integrity of their work and the compassionate love that it demonstrated. Linemen and quarterbacks – what a combination!

These were some of the ripples from the work of Weavers of Hope that I could see and identify. I know that there were others which I never saw, and I'm OK with that. And, I suspect that there will be many more to come as the work goes on. We have not yet reached the edges of the pond. What a joyous and hopeful thought that is.

# Weavers of Hope Sponsored Students

Outside Casa Clemens (circa 2009)
Holding stuffed animal gifts from a sponsor

Parents and children enjoying a student presentation at a monthly meeting
(inside Casa Clemens)

Outside Casa Clemens
Students gather to thank their sponsors after a monthly meeting

Lupe (chapter 6) with grandbaby

Julieta (center) with two members of the Parents Committee
Rosalba on left and Lupe on right

Holy Week pilgrimage, outside Villa Garcia

Inside Fran's home
Fran (left) and Julieta – planning the strategy for a Weavers of Hope student gathering

Lupe, the weaver, at work on his loom

Locally woven rugs from Villa Garci

Preparing to leave Austin, Texas, on a mission awareness trip to Villa Garcia
Al (standing); Left to right: Wolf, Marianne, Martha, Jack, Wayne

Distributing clothes and treats from Kay
Kay (left) with children in Villa Garcia

Chole & Rosalia present reports to Kay & Jack for the "$900 Project"
Left to right: Kay, Chole, Rosalia, Jack

After a Saint Vincent de Paul meeting in Villa Garcia. Local chapter – formed in 2003 to do social outreach to the needy
Martha, the caretaker of Casa Clemens, is front row, far right

Intensive, two-week English workshop in Casa Clemens (Summer 2010)
Students learning English vocabulary as Mateo plays guitar and everyone sings 'Let It Be' by the Beatles

*"Lasting change happens when people see for themselves that a different way of life is more fulfilling than their present one."*

**Eknath Easwaran**

# Visions and Dreams

When I leave my home in south Austin, I often pass a white truck parked on a street in my neighborhood with large letters that say UBUNTU on the back windshield. My curiosity was piqued the first time I saw this strange word. On subsequent trips, I slowed down to read the smaller print below UBUNTU which read, "I am because we are." I smiled as I thought of the similarity in meaning between this word and *Una Familia Humana* – One Human Family.

The internet told me that the word had its origin in the Bantu languages of southern Africa. It is an ethical and humanistic philosophy which focuses on people's allegiances and relationships with each other. Archbishop Desmond Tutu offered this definition in a 1999 book:

*"A person with Ubuntu is open and available to others, affirming of others, does not feel threatened that others are able and good, for he or she has a proper self-assurance that comes from knowing that he or she belongs in a greater whole and is diminished when others are humiliated or diminished, when others are tortured or oppressed."*

Another derivative of the Ubuntu philosophy offers guidance on how to behave and interact in various social roles. It talks of the highest standards of behavior and respect for all other people. Some African applications of the word take it a step further. They say that children are never orphans because the roles of mothers and fathers are, by definition, not vested in a single individual with respect to a single child. The applications of Ubuntu are strongly supportive of respect, peace, togetherness, and justice.

In 2009, U.S. Department of State Special Representative for Global Partnerships, Elizabeth Bagley, discussed Ubuntu in the context of American foreign policy. She said:

*"In understanding the responsibilities that come with our interconnectedness, we realize that we must rely on each other to lift our world from where it is now to where we want it to be in our lifetime, while casting aside our worn out preconceptions, and our outdated modes of statecraft."*

Ms. Bagley went on to introduce the notion of "Ubuntu Diplomacy". She stressed the importance of bringing people together from across regions and sectors to work in partnerships on issues of common interest. She spoke of the U.S. being a catalyst in launching new projects in tandem with non-governmental organizations, philanthropists, and corporations that are on the front lines of foreign affairs work. She challenged all of the partners in this effort to work in unity to discover untapped potential, inspire fresh ideas, and create new solutions.

In summarizing Ubuntu Diplomacy, Ms. Bagley offered this definition:

*"…where all sectors belong as partners, where we all participate as stakeholders, and where we all succeed together, not incrementally but exponentially."*

The Boston Celtics, the 2008 National Basketball Association champions, have chanted "Ubuntu" when breaking a huddle since the start of the 2007-2008 season. Ubuntu was a major theme in John Boorman's 2004 film "In My Country". At the 2002 United Nations World Summit on Sustainable Development, there was an Ubuntu Village exposition center.

It struck me that Ubuntu philosophies are at the core of what drives Weavers of Hope. Like Elizabeth Bagley's dreams of a new kind of American foreign policy, Weavers of Hope leaders have visions and dreams of closer connections with the Mexican people. In these dreams we are partners who succeed together.

In humanitarian work and social partnerships there is always a temptation to widen the scope and try to do more. The needs are great, and the people who do this work desperately want to make a difference. However, good organizations seem never to lose their focus. They are careful not to over-extend. They know what their basic mission is, and they stay true to that scope.

Our basic missions in order of importance at Weavers of Hope are two-fold:
1. We believe that education is an outstanding way to achieve long-term change, both for the individual and for the culture. Approximately 80-90% of what we do is focused in this area.
2. The rest of our work is focused almost exclusively on expanding the concepts of fair trade for the weavers of Villa Garcia. By design, this is a second, smaller project.

That is not to say that there will never be a third focus or that the percentage splits won't be adjusted. But it is to say clearly that we know what our scope and focus is at this time. It also says that we will be very careful and conscious before making any changes to our basic mission. We want to accomplish our mission with a high degree of integrity, caring, and quality.

I mentioned earlier in the book that we are modeled after the Christian Foundation for Children and Aging, a large, successful, non-profit organization with a similar educational focus. We have learned a lot from that organization.

So, what are our visions and dreams for our main focus, the Weavers of Hope educational sponsorship program?

At the core of our dreams is working in partnerships to foster the philosophies of UBUNTU and *Una Familia Humana* – One Human Family. Specifically, we hope to do this primarily by building relationships of trust and caring between the sponsors, workers, students, and families in Weavers of Hope.

It is our hope to accomplish this vision by working together to provide educational opportunities for young people. We have seen visible signs of the ripple effects from the education of our Weavers of Hope students.

Here's what some of our university graduates are doing:
- Eliseo is an accountant for a large company in Mexico – he helps to pay for his younger brother's education.
- Magda a is a special education teacher in Villa Garcia.
- Antonio and Octavio (engineering degrees) have opened an internet business.
- Chuy (masters in counseling) travels to Villa Garcia on Saturdays to provide family counseling.
- Theresa (9 years in the convent before receiving a psychology degree) conducted a retreat workshop for children in Villa Garcia in 2010.
- Juan Carlos, a teacher in a rural area, returned to do an inspirational talk to the current Weavers of Hope students.

These graduates are making a difference in the lives of others, and in their community. However, the needs in Villa Garcia, the surrounding areas, the state of Zacatecas, and beyond are enormous. People are struggling to survive, and many young people are without the means to continue their education.

We need many more sponsors. We invite you to become a Weavers of Hope sponsor. If you are able to sponsor a student, it would be a tremendous help (see appendix one for how to contact Weavers of Hope). Please consider inviting other family members and friends to become sponsors. Perhaps your family could share a sponsorship as a part of your holiday season. Maybe there are other ways you could help us to find new sponsors.

One of the primary ways that we encounter new sponsors is by telling the stories of our work. If you are connected to a faith community, civic organization, social group, work community, or any other group, we would love the opportunity to speak with your group about the work of Weavers of Hope. Setting us up to speak and to share the stories would be a huge help.

I smile when I think about requesting speaking engagements. When I left my paying job at Shell Oil Company, one of the things I most looked forward to was never having to give another presentation. They always made me nervous. I read in a poll once that most people fear public speaking more than death. And now, here I am, asking for the opportunity to speak to large groups of people all over the nation, and beyond. I think that God must have a sense of humor.

The publishing of this book provides a really exciting opportunity for getting the Weavers of Hope story out to a wider audience. It allows us to honor the hard-working families and students of Villa Garcia. I've enjoyed being able to chronicle the events that led up to this work. It has been fulfilling to remember our roots, to review where we currently stand, and to share our visions and dreams for the future.

During the writing of this book, something else has been birthed in me. I'm not sure where it came from, but it feels very good. I have been given the beginnings of the gift of detachment. The joy of writing this story stands on its own, and is not dependent on any tangible results that may occur.

Detachment does not in any way imply that I care less. I care passionately about this work and about promoting the concepts of UBUNTU and *Una Familia Humana* – One Human Family. The concepts of unity resonate at the deepest levels of my being. However, when this book has been published and distributed, I know that the results will be in God's hands. This feeling of detachment helps me to remember my place as a servant and worker who is only a small cog in an immensely larger grand plan.

You can be a part of whatever results from the publishing of this book by helping us to distribute it to individuals and groups. You can help us to find new readers who might enjoy reliving this experience with us. If each person who reads this book passes it on to another person who might read it, we can double our audience. If you belong to a book club, you might suggest this book for your group to read.

Do you know of an organization that provides grants to assist organizations who focus on helping Mexican students to continue their education? Can you get us the names of foundations, corporations, groups, or individuals who share our vision of UBUNTU through educational opportunities for Mexican students? For those organizations or individuals with whom you have a professional or personal relationship, can you provide a letter of introduction and support for Weavers of Hope? We would be excited to apply for grants that have a reasonable chance of success.

One of the greatest ways for people to see and experience the work of Weavers of Hope is by visiting Villa Garcia, and meeting Fran, Julieta, the students, and their families. Are you connected to a group who might consider making a mission awareness trip with us?

We would also welcome any donations that you would make to support our work. Please also consider leaving a legacy gift to Weavers of Hope through wills, trusts, life insurance, or other tangible assets. Contact us for more details on this option.

These are some of our visions and dreams for UBUNTU, *Una Familia Humana* – One Human Family, solidarity, and long-term change. Will you join us in some capacity to help to make these dreams a reality?

The second focus of Weavers of Hope, after the educational sponsorship program, is to expand the markets for fair trade weavings. There are many weaving families in Villa Garcia, like Lupe's in the last chapter, who could lift themselves out of poverty if these markets were further developed. Our vision is to do this, and to restore Villa Garcia to a position of prominence in the weaving industry.

Oaxaca, Mexico has done this. Located in the far southern part of the country, they have become world famous for their weavings. They have developed the markets, established the reputation, and provided for their long-term sustainability. We can do the same thing in Villa Garcia. We can study what they did to reach this level of success and learn from it.

The weaving project, as we envision it, is clearly a business venture. However, it is a business that will be built solidly on the principles of fair trade. Workers will not be exploited or isolated. Rather, they will be paid just wages, encouraged to build cooperatives, and given incentives to work in environmentally friendly ways. Profits will help to maintain the weaving infrastructure and will be shared by the workers. A significant percentage of the profits will continue to be funneled into the educational sponsorship program of Weavers of Hope. This will help to provide long-term sustainability for both the weavers and the students.

So, what do we need to do this? We need volunteers with a wide variety of skills and talents. We need you. First of all we need a project manager(s) with significant business and personal skills. We need a team of talented people. The vision needs to be developed in conjunction with the local weavers of Villa Garcia. The cooperatives need to be formed and nurtured. This will require the concept of UBUNTU, connectedness, and a determination that we work together for the benefit of everyone.

After forming the cooperatives, we need to get fair trade certification. This certification guarantees consumers that strict economic, social, and environmental criteria were met in the production and trade of a product.

With this certification, we will be able to partner with various organizations that promote fair trade products. Markets, especially in the U.S., will need to be developed, websites built, and shipping facilities established. Product lines will need to be developed with local workers being able to produce everything. The current product line of rugs, wall hangings, and ponchos will need to be expanded to include purses, belts, backpacks, computer cases, and other products that have high demand levels.

It's exciting, isn't it? There are readers of this book who have the exact talents that we need to accomplish this dream. Some of them have time in their lives and may be thinking about doing some type of humanitarian work. Here is an opportunity to work on a project that can change lives and do an enormous amount of good. If this vision gets your juices flowing, please join our team. We need your energy, passion, vision, and talents. We can work together with the weavers of Villa Garcia to make this dream a reality. We can help families to move themselves from poverty to security.

Over the years since beginning Weavers of Hope we have been blessed with many wonderful volunteers who have sponsored students, visited Villa Garcia, sold weavings, sponsored garage sales, and told our story. Others have helped with bookkeeping, accounting, tax preparation, legal matters, newsletter preparation, music videos, website development, mail outs, sponsor communications, and building databases to support the organization. The tasks are many and the volunteers are too numerous to mention by name. But each one of them is a significant part of our success and where we are today.

As we go forward, all of these tasks will continue to grow in size, magnitude, and complexity. These are wonderful problems to have. They are the result of a growing, vibrant organization.

We need a creative webmaster with the vision for how best to utilize the power of the internet. Social networking sites like Facebook need to be incorporated into the Weavers of Hope business plan. There is a future potential for selling t-shirts, caps, mugs, mouse pads, and a variety of other products. These are opportunities waiting to be explored.

The other side of the coin is that we need more dedicated volunteers to join in doing this work. We also need fresh ideas for how to do things better. If you have an interest in fostering UBUNTU by working to help a young organization to grow and prosper, we need you.

Finally, it would be wonderful if someone would volunteer to translate this book into Spanish.

I would like to conclude with a personal story that focuses on *la balanza*, the balance, in life. The necessity of staying in balance is slowly being revealed to me. Maybe a better way to say it is that I am finally open to having these concepts revealed to me.

When I left my paying job at Shell Oil Company, I made a long list of things that I would love to do in the next phase of my life. They included travel, adventure, new experiences, opening a business, growing in spirituality, and a wide variety of other things. I wanted to do different things, even though I wasn't exactly sure what they were. The transition into retirement had me feeling an immense level of freedom. There were so many exciting options to choose from.

I tried a number of things with varying levels of success. However, the really big step away from Shell Oil and into a new lifestyle was when I said yes to being a part of the JustFaith class on social justice in 2001. That was the definable moment for me, the moment when a new vision of the world began to become clear.

In biblical terminology, it was when the scales fell from my eyes. I had not seen, or chosen not to see, how social issues can force people into poverty. This vision led to radical changes in many parts of my life. I emerged from JustFaith bubbling over with energy and passion, and wanting to make a difference in the world.

After beginning Weavers of Hope, Martha and I moved into central Austin. Many new opportunities to work for social justice arose. We joined a vibrant faith community which was dedicated to working for and promoting justice in our community and beyond. Before committing to the parish, we spent two hours talking with Sean, the Pastoral Associate, at Saint Ignatius, Martyr Catholic Church in south Austin. He laid out a vision for the social mission of the church which rang true to me.

During this conversation, I knew instinctively that Sean would be creative, energizing, and fun to work with. All of that has proved to be true beyond my best dreams. We have become friends, spiritual companions, and co-workers on a variety of social justice issues. Through these projects, I have met many more caring, passionately committed people. They have brought rich friendships, diverse talents, and much laughter into my life.

I used to go to church on Sunday, then bolt for the doors and the afternoon football games on TV. Now, I hang around because there are so many people that I love to talk with. I've never had such a beautiful sense of belonging to a community.

I have talked about the experiences which shaped me after JustFaith in earlier chapters of the book. The thing I did not talk about was the other activities that I immersed myself in beyond Weavers of Hope and teaching English as a Second Language (ESL).

Justice education, community organizing, planning social justice conferences, and leadership roles in the social outreach projects of my faith community consumed my time and energy. When those new projects were added onto the work of Weavers of Hope and ESL it was too much. It was the classic case of trying to save the world, and there is no doubt that amidst the good, there was a generous sprinkling of pride and ego. Self-righteousness became an ugly part of who I was. And, the strange thing is that I never saw it creeping in.

Martha is always gentle with me and gives me a lot of room to run, be excited, and chase my dreams. She also knows when it is time to reel me in because I have gone too far. This was one of those times when she asked me to step back and look at the bigger picture of my life. I could begin to see that I was overcommitted, and the trend was to continue to take on new things. That mode of operation was not sustainable.

In my times of prayer it became clear to me that Martha's cautions were filled with wisdom and love. My life was out of balance. I'm convinced that it was these times of prayer that kept me from going totally off the deep end. Yet, even with that divine help, I was walking on the edge of the cliff.

One of my favorite speakers and authors is a Franciscan priest named Richard Rohr. His writings and talks gave me more insights into striving for balance in life. Rohr founded The Center for Action and Contemplation in Albuquerque, New Mexico. As the name implies, his organization is dedicated to keeping the balance between prayer and action. The prayer form that he most often talked about was contemplative or meditative prayer.

Along with the teachings of Richard Rohr and several others, I began to get new insights from reading the gospels. I saw a Jesus who was a very social person. He spent time with people from all walks of life, e.g. religious leaders, government officials, women, fishermen, sinners, tax collectors, prostitutes, friends, and the people He taught. Jesus focused on justice, fairness, and structures in society which gave each human being an opportunity to flourish and enjoy life. He challenged both religious and secular leaders to work for compassionate societies with justice for all. I also saw a Jesus who consistently took time out to pray. Prayer and action, just like Richard Rohr's center in New Mexico. I began to see more clearly my need for both.

I was heavier into the action piece than I was into the prayer part. However, I was trying to achieve a better balance. In the middle of all these thoughts, stirrings, and movements, I wandered into a Centering Prayer meeting, not sure exactly what to expect. I knew that this prayer practice seemed to fit into what I would have called meditation. I yearned for more stillness and quiet time in my life. I had had a serious, committed prayer life prior to this time, but it was not a daily prayer practice. All of that would change.

I learned that Centering Prayer is a method of quiet and emptying that prepares a person to receive the gift of contemplative prayer from God. If God grants the gift, it is the opening of mind and heart, our whole being, to God, the Ultimate Mystery, beyond thoughts words, and emotions. I fell in love with this prayer practice immediately. For the first time in my life, I felt like I had come home to the place of prayer where I belonged.

I joined Contemplative Outreach, Limited, a spiritual network of individuals and small faith communities committed to living the contemplative traditions. I began to devour a variety of books on Centering Prayer, many written by Thomas Keating, one of the founders of Contemplative Outreach, Limited. I was hungry to learn more of the history, philosophy, and experiences of others who have done this prayer for many years.

I had all of the typical questions that beginners ask. I also needed a sounding board for the types of experiences that I was having. I had no idea what to expect from this type of prayer, but I did know that intuitively it felt right. My hunger for continuing this prayer form was as intense as my hunger for working to promote social justice. Prayer and action were coming together in my own life, and I felt noticeably grounded, perhaps more so than ever before.

The leader of our weekly Centering Prayer meetings is a wonderful man named Mike. He has become a treasured friend and spiritual companion. Eventually, I began to stay after the weekly meetings to talk with Mike. He was honest, easy to talk with, and freely shared his story with me. He also listened intently when I talked about what I was experiencing. Then, he kindly asked for permission to comment on what I had said. He has been my sounding board for over five years now, and our friendship continues to grow.

Prayer, action/work, and quality time with my family and friends has become the mix that has helped to keep me in balance. Almost every day begins the same, lovely way for me. I arise early, make coffee, go to my prayer space, light a couple of candles, and put on some incense. That sets the mood. I begin with some type of spiritual reading, followed by Centering Prayer. Then, I connect with Martha for our time of conversation and prayer together. This works beautifully for me. When I don't get that start to the day, I feel uncomfortable and off balance, like I have not brushed my teeth.

In no way do I think that I have "arrived", nor do I ever expect to "arrive". But, I do know that I'm on the journey, flawed as it is, and I'm OK with just knowing that. I am learning to forgive myself for the many things that I do wrong, especially the things that hurt others or myself. I trust in the infinite forgiveness of my God. And, I pick myself up and try again to live an honorable life.

My heart goes out to the good people of Mexico who are living during these times of civil war between the drug cartels, increasing violence, and the breakdown of an orderly society. The stories of killings, torture, and kidnappings dominate the news. You can almost feel the creeping terror in the honest, hard-working citizens of Mexico. There is no end in sight to these problems.

Villa Garcia is still a peaceful community, but many of those who live there have family members and friends who live in different parts of the country. Often, these family members and friends are trapped in the escalating horrors of the drug wars.

Weavers of Hope provides families with a glimmer of hope for themselves and their children. Parents still dream that with education their children will be able to live lives of dignity and peace. Our work is like a tiny light in what sometimes seems like an overwhelming darkness. I am intensely honored to be a small part of that light and hope.

APPENDIX 1
# Contact Information

Below is a list of the major organizations that are mentioned in this book along with their contact information.

**Weavers of Hope**
Website:  www.weaversofhope.org
Jack:  kern.jack@gmail.com
         512-947-4775 or 512-320-0996
         1011 Brodie Street, Unit 8
         Austin, Texas  78704

**JustFaith Ministries**
Website:  www.justfaith.org

**Christian Foundation for Children and Aging (CFCA)**
Website:  www.cfcausa.org

**Contemplative Outreach**
Website:  www.contemplativeoutreach.org

APPENDIX 2
# Student Sketches
BY: SR. FRAN SMITH

## Liliana

Liliana was a very talented but frequently sick student. She was not in school when she solicited help, as she was getting over a bout of typhoid fever and did not have the resourses to continue her studies in the university, though she was determined to do so. She was always working to help the family and to be able to continue her studies.

Liliana was able to go back to the university but needed lots of extra help, as expenses were great. She had a sponsor who sent her many useful items, especially after she had her first child. But Liliana did finish, did her service requirement work in a laboratory in Villa Garcia, later worked there, and now lives with her husband and two children in Aguascalientes.

Liliana was one of the leaders of the students receiving grants. She didn't hesitate to take over the leadership of the meetings. After she finished her studies in pharmaceutical chemistry and biology, she would help folks by giving advice on how to handle certain health problems. Always willing, always cheerful, we rejoiced that she could finish her professional studies.

## Eliseo

When Eliseo was six years old his father asked him if he wanted to have therapy or get an education. Eliseo was born with deformed arms and legs and chose education. When I met him he was studying accounting. I learned that he had tried other fields in the university, but they hadn't worked out. With four siblings in school the family was struggling to keep Eliseo in the university. Eliseo needed help with things we take for granted, like getting in and out of public transportation. He needed money for taxis in the city, as he couldn't board the buses. He needed English, so he was given classes here in my house. He was a natural with the language, and when he applied for his first job after graduating, he knew enough English to get hired as a supervisor selling products.

This job was short-lived, and before we knew it he was working a government job in accounting. After several years he began working for the large Corona company, where he presently works. He recounts how he had his first plane trip through this company which flew him to Mexico City to prepare him for his work.

Eliseo was an umpire for his rural community's baseball games when we first met him. Every week he could be found on the baseball field, so it wasn't surprising that when Jack came last year and wanted to talk to him that we found him on a remote field, this time in Villa Garcia, where his team was playing. Eliseo is a good example of someone whose life has been changed because he chose education, his family sacrificed so he could get it, and Weavers of Hope gave a helping hand when it was most needed. But his story doesn't end here, for Eliseo is now sponsoring his brother in the university. And so the ministry goes on and is bearing fruit.

## Magdalena

Magda wanted to be a special education teacher, but she didn't have the family financial support needed. Four siblings were in school besides her; her father was a teacher, but a serious alcoholic at the time. Weavers of Hope gave Magda the opportunity to continue her studies. She was an excellent student and helped with special needs children when asked to. She graduated, found work in her field, albeit far away as many beginning teachers do, and began to take advanced classes on her own. She found work closer after those first two years, and now is in Villa Garcia provisionally, working with the schools that have special needs children. I saw Magda when we celebrated Children's Day here this year. Magda was with the newly-opened and rapidly growing Special Ed school in Villa Garcia. She is a natural with these children and hopes to get permanent work in the village. She is married and has two children and makes her home in Villa Garcia. Magda is a good example of someone who is bringing her talent and education back to the village, thus enriching the lives of all and giving back to her own community.

## Mayra Alejandra

Mayra was a fifth grader when she entered the program. Of the ten children in the house, four others were in school. Her father was a brick maker, a job that depends on the dry season for work. Mayra's goal was to be a teacher. None of her older sisters had continued in school, but Mayra wanted this opportunity.

Mayra did continue and went on to junior high, leaving school after ninth grade. However, she was the first in her family to make it this far, and this was a good reason to celebrate. Mayra is now married, also to a brick maker, has one child, and seems to be a mature young woman at age 20. She is an active member of our pastoral social committee, thus giving back to the community in ways one could not have imagined eight years ago. She also actively recruits for the Weavers of Hope program, introducing us to some of the neediest families.

## Ricardo

I recall so well the day I interviewed Ricardo. His father was a weaver, part of a new cooperative being formed. His mother helped an elderly, bedridden woman. Ricardo liked making bricks when he wasn't in school and planned to do so for the rest of his life. The family income totaled around $80 a month. He was in his final year of high school and his grades weren't very good. He needed glasses, had broken them, and didn't have the money to get them replaced.

Helping Ricardo do better in school was our first goal. He entered the program and began to look at options he might like to pursue, finally choosing human rights. Ricardo continued to struggle to maintain good grades in the university, and only when his average fell below a B for two semesters was he forced to leave the program. He continued, however, with his studies. He found part-time work in a factory and was able to continue until his last year when the financial crisis hit Mexico. His parents were then selling fresh juices and snacks and weren't making enough to help him out. Ricardo is now working at odd jobs, still hoping to save enough money to finish his degree. He needs glasses once again, has been without them for three years. He isn't making enough money to replace them, much less save up for the university. His grade point average is still a bit below B. Ricardo wonders if he'll ever be able to finish his studies. Everyone hopes he'll be able to, both for Ricardo, for his parents, and for Villa Garcia.

## Antonio

Antonio was about to leave high school when his employer, a construction worker, suggested we check him out for a grant. His grades were low, we discovered, because he spent all his free time working in order to graduate. When we began helping Antonio, everything changed. His grades were good and he began exploring the means for continuing his studies. Antonio chose to be an electrical engineer, graduating in this field. The year he graduated his father, a diabetic, went blind. The family moved to the city of Zacatecas in order to take him to the doctor more easily.

There, Antonio, along with a companion, Octavio, began by setting up a cyber (internet business), which became their chief means of income. Antonio works in his field when called upon, but there hasn't been full time work for him in engineering. He supports the family by stocking the little grocery store his mother runs and by sponsoring his younger brother.

Antonio was always a leader in the group. He counseled one of the other boys when Jose's parents separated. He was responsible for recruiting others in need of grants. He would share what he'd learned with anyone needing his help. On the side he worked at selling natural health products so that he could help his family and others who had health problems. Like most of our students, however, he doesn't live nearby anymore, for there is little or no work in the isolated village of Villa Garcia. However, his influence is still felt and he is responsive when contacted.

## Maria Susana

Susana is one of the first students I met. She was in high school and needed some help with English. Her mother ran a small store, her father worked in the chicken factory, and her brother sometimes found work in the U.S. The family lived in a small space behind the store, lent them by her grandfather's family. As with many families, a bath was taken by warming water in a bucket and throwing the water over one. The family had built a loft so Susana would have a place to sleep.

Susana was one of our early leaders, able to speak in front of the group and help get them organized. She would be the first ever to become a professional in her family. Attending her graduation from normal school (teacher training school) was a thrill for all of us. In Mexico, finding a place to teach can be tiresome, as all is done on a seniority basis. One's name is added to a list of those waiting for an assignment. One checks in at headquarters on designated days and waits for the day there is an opening.

When those first assignments are given, they are frequently for a three-month leave for a pregnant teacher. Then there might be a year where some teacher is on a sabbatical, etc. Finally, after several years one is given a permanent place in the lineup. Sometimes a political contact or a teacher in the family helps move the process along. Since Susana had no one in the family to make the process go faster, she has been happy to simply have a job. She has been taking courses in psychology to advance in her career and hopes to get her masters some day. Always cheerful and full of life, she is happy to be able to help her family. She helps her mother stock her store and has been able to help her brother, now married and living in her former nook in the loft.

## Jesus (Chuy)

Chuy is the youngest of twelve children of an indigenous family from the state of Michoacan. He had recently left the novitiate of a religious order and gone to Aguascalientes to be near his brother Emilio who lived there with his family. He entered the university in Aguascalientes and began his studies in psychology. As he could not stay with his brother's family, he ended up at Caritas, the Aguascalientes Diocese's equivalent of Catholic Charities. When I met Chuy he was working three jobs and taking classes at the university. The director of the *prepa abierta,* open high school, where I was a volunteer, Sister Blanca Margarita, told me that they were giving him a room in which to live and providing him with some meals each day. However, she said, he needed help with his school costs.

Chuy was getting only about three hours of sleep a day with his busy schedule. We were just beginning our grant program and didn't know how it would work out to have someone from outside the local area of Villa Garcia and vicinity. However, we decided to risk it. And what a blessed risk it has been! Chuy no longer had to work three jobs. He worked only two, got more rest, and did better in his studies.

One time when Chuy went to see his family in Michoacan he had a minor surgery performed on his sinuses. When he got back to Aguascalientes he began to have problems with his left arm. It was becoming paralyzed, and as Chuy worked as a waiter, this was serious. Incredibly, he continued his work, as he needed the income to continue his studies, visited any number of doctors and had his arm in a cast up to his fingers, which were also immobile. Eventually he found a therapist that helped him get his feeling back, spending many hours dealing with this health problem.

Chuy not only graduated on time, he also had good enough grades that he didn't have to write an extra thesis. He wanted to give back to the community that had helped him and set up a counseling schedule in Villa Garcia on Saturdays. Some months later he began on his masters, with a specialty in family counseling. He graduated two years later with a 10 or 100% in his studies. He is always looking for ways to give back to the program. He has given two workshops for the parent committee of Weavers of Hope, several talks to the university students in the program, and every Saturday he has counseling sessions with folks who are very pleased with the help he's been giving.

Chuy has had work most of the time since he's graduated. He continues to take specialized courses to be able to help in a broader manner. He knew a new kind of freedom when he was able to purchase his first used car. For some months this year he's had to use public transportation, but he hasn't missed a beat as far as service is concerned. Chuy is giving back to our community in a most significant manner, one we couldn't have foreseen and for which we are most appreciative. He has become a role model for the others we are sponsoring and is always willing to talk to Weavers of Hope about his experiences, about his values, and about what he has learned.

## Armando

We became acquainted with Armando when the first JustFaith group came to visit Villa Garcia in 2003. Armando's sister asked the group for help for her family, as they were about to lose their home to a man they owed money to. The father of the family had gone to the United States to work and not returned nor been in contact. Armando's mom had given up the title to the house when she borrowed needed money. The house was about to be reclaimed.

As Armando was the oldest boy in the family and wanted to continue his studies, we gave him a grant to remain in high school. After high school he wanted to study history, but because of few economic resources he entered a local technical school. He did not do well in this school and left to work awhile. The next year he entered the university to study history. Armando is now in his final years of study, doing well, loves history, and plans to teach when he is finished with his studies.

## Teresa

Teresa was in the convent for nine years and decided to leave to study psychology. A leader in her community, Aguagordita, she was a catechist and involved in every level of community action there. When she asked for a grant to finish her studies, she was a mature young woman and determined to be good in whatever she attempted. She graduated, found work, and got married. Teresa continues to be an inspiration to all who know her, helping out in her rural village when she visits. She conducted a retreat workshop for children this year and gave a retreat conference at Casa Clemens. Teresa is always willing to give back to the community, and is helping many people with her gifts.

# Juan Carlos

Teresa introduced us to Juan Carlos, her cousin. Juan's brother grew up in Teresa's home, as Juan's mother died when he and his brothers and sister were young. Eventually the father remarried a wonderful stepmother who cared for the remaining family members. Juan wanted to get a degree in photography and enrolled in the university for this. He was forced to leave, as he could not keep up with the payments. We met Juan a few months after this. Juan decided to enter a normal, teacher training school, as the costs were less and grants were available in these schools.

Juan has always been a leader among the students. He would make suggestions to Jack and Fran about ways to make the program better. Eventually, he was in charge of reviewing how the grant money was being spent by the students. Now Juan is a successful teacher in a very poor, rural area. He helped organize the village so they could have transportation in and out of the village several days a week. He may not be reassigned to this village, but he's left his mark and is proud of it. Recently, he shared his experiences as a grantee and now as a teacher with the entire Weavers of Hope group. He wants to continue to be a part of the group, and is planting the seeds for the continued growth of the organization.

APPENDIX 3

# Student Letters

Below are some letters that the Weavers of Hope students have written to their sponsors. Before Weavers of Hope, many of these students had never written letters like these. Through workshops and personal guidance provided by Fran and Julieta, they are now better able to express themselves in writing.

Dear Sponsor,

Hello - hope you are well. During this semester I did very well even though the work load was a little heavier!

Currently, I am doing my professional practices. For this, my teammates and I go to a retirement home in Guadalupe, Zacatecas. We've been on 6 visits so far. It is very nice to work with older people. It has been an experience that has really impacted me. I have realized that the elderly have great energy and desire to continue living. During each visit we are received with great joy. We spend about two hours with the people living in the Home, taking part in and organizing activities with them. The activities help motivate them to feel useful and loved. We make rosaries and bracelets, paint clay figurines, and also hold dance contests. The people there love the activities. Sometimes it's sad because you realize that the people who live at the Home have been abandoned. The visits are bittersweet.

On October 29 we organized a contest of altars and costumes to celebrate the Day of the Dead and everything was really cool. I had fun.

My family and I have been well thanks to God. My dad is still sick though. He has a blood disease and is in treatment. I do not know how long he will be in treatment, but hopefully soon he will be better.

No more for now. Wishing you all the best!
Ana

Hello Sponsors,

I hope you and your family are well. I am very happy to be able to write to you again.

Now that my sister Brenda and I are on vacation, we are in charge of the house and taking care of our siblings while my mom works. I am very excited about this because I believe that Christmas is the season to be with family. It is also a time, for me, which conjures up many memories from when I was a child. One of my best memories was waiting for the Niño Dios[1]. Every Christmas Eve, I told my family I was going to stay awake to see and talk to the Niño Dios, but was never able to make good on my claims. I fell asleep every year! ☺ I always woke up the next day, as early as I could, to see the gifts he had brought. I think the best gift I ever received from the Niño Dios was a doll with brown hair that looked like me.

I wish you a Merry Christmas and a happy New Year. I also hope that one day you can come for Christmas to meet my family. My house is very humble, but the doors are always open for you and your family.

Sincerely,
Ericka

PS - thanks again for all your support.

---

1 El Niño de Dios is the Mexican equivalent to the U.S. Santa Claus. Translated El Niño de Dios means "The son of God." Many parents in Mexico, especially in the small pueblos, prefer that their children believe in El Niño de Dios instead of Santa because they feel it maintains the Catholic significance of Christmas.

Hello, Sponsor!

I hope you are well. I want to begin by saying that I am new to the Weavers of Hope program. I started in August of this year. My name is Evangelina. I am 20 years old and I'm studying biological chemistry at la Univerisdad Autónoma de Aguascalientes. I just finished my 3rd semester. My main goals are to finish my career, work in a laboratory, and teach middle school.

In my free time I like to read science fiction novels. Some of my favorite books are from the Harry Potter series. I like them because they are about hidden creatures and magic.

My family is made up of six people. My dad, Joel is an electrician, but for the moment doesn't have work. He has applications in mining companies and has been promised some small jobs next year. He has worked sporadically and with this he supports us. My mom's name is Alicia. She is a housewife and seamstress. She makes clothes, when she can, and sells them to help support my family. I have two sisters, the first is named Guadalupe. She is 15. Maria Claudia is 8 years old. Lastly, I have a brother who is 2 years old. I hope someday to hear about your family

My family and I plan to make a steak with beans and guacamole for Christmas dinner. We put up a very nice nativity, as well as a tree.

Recently, we celebrated the feast day of Our Lady of Guadalupe on the 12th of December. Pilgrimages were made to Villa Garcia from small surrounding communities during the 11 days prior to the feast day. One Friday we took part in the pilgrimage and my sister Maria Claudia road a float dressed as the Virgin Mary. She was in the middle of a flower surrounded by girls who were dressed as angels. When the feast day came my family and I went to see fireworks. They were beautiful and we had a good time.

Finally, I want to thank you for the opportunity to have a scholarship to help pay my tuition and school expenses. Thanks to your support I have the possibility to graduate. Someday I will be able to work to help my parents like they have helped me. I hope you liked what I wrote and that you have gotten to known me a little by reading the letter.

Take care - Evangelina

Hello dear sponsor.

I hope that this finds you in good health, and I also hope that your whole family is with you during this special time.

I want to thank "Weavers of Hope" because I am new to the program. My name is Mayra. I live in Villa Garcia, and have three siblings that are younger than me. I'm in college, studying for a BA in history. My school is located in the city of Zacatecas, but I spend my weekends in Villa Garcia with my family. Going away to college was very different, but I like it. The support that I receive from you has helped me to get ahead and to keep up with my financial obligations. I do not know my most recent GPA yet, but I hope to have achieved good results. My goals are to finish my degree and to teach.

Let me share with you my relationship I have with my family. It is the engine that drives me forward. My relationship with my parents and siblings is very good. We talk and spend time together. I hope your relationship with your family is also good. I would like you to share something about your family with me.

In these days for Christmas my family gets together, we give gifts and remember good things from throughout the year, nice moments we spent together. This is part of our culture here in Mexico. How is it there? How do you celebrate Christmas? I am interested in your culture and if the festivities are the same as here.

I am pleased to write this letter and especially to maintain communication with you so I can thank you for the support you are providing me. This support is important for me, because with it I can stay in school. Thank you for taking time to read this letter. Thank you and goodbye.

Sincerely,
Mayra

To my dear sponsor,

It is a pleasure for me to write these few lines and share with you what has been happening during these past few months. First of all, I want to thank you for the generous support you give me. Please know that this financial support will be invested in my professional development and my commitment to help others.

Time goes by soo fast! Here in Villa Garcia we have already had our celebration dedicated to the Virgin of Guadalupe. The celebration included a nightly rosary, pilgrimages, parades, fireworks, and more. I hope you have a Merry Christmas and a Happy New Year filled with health and wellness.

Changing the subject a bit, I want to share with you what has been going on in school. I have had a lot of work during this last semester and have felt a bit weighted down with the responsibilities of my professional practice. I am doing my practicum in an organization called Screen IT. My tasks include seeking qualified professional resumes for positions in Information Technology. I help search for candidates looking for job vacancies in companies such as HCL, General Electric.

I also have a class called Intercultural Communication, and we are responsible for a project proposal for a community or organization. I have worked with Julieta on my project proposal using Weavers of Hope as my organization.

The major focus of my proposal is to improve communication between scholarship students and their sponsors. I have first suggested creating a space on the organization's website, where we (the scholarship students) can share photos of achievements in school, our family and friends, projects, events in our community, etc. The major problem that we face is language. We are told that most of you do not speak Spanish and we do not speak English. I don't know how many sponsors use the network of Facebook, but I have discussed this as an option as well.

I hope you like my suggestions and if you think of anything more appropriate I would love to know. You can send us your comments in Spanish or English.

In the meantime, I will send you some pictures of my project prototypes: the quarterly brochure in Spanish, facebook profile, and an interactive blog.

Sincerely,
Nayeli

◆ ◆ ◆

Hello!

I am really happy to be able to write to you again and to let you know what has been happening in my life. I hope that you and your family are doing well and that you have enjoyed a very restful and enjoyable holiday.

During the holidays I reflect a lot on the times I have spent with my family. Especially the times I spent with my father. He's not with us in the physical sense, but he is surely here in spirit. I am sure he is also looking down with a lot of pride for what my sister and I are doing. Thank you for helping to make this possible.

As you know I am coming very close to the end of my university studies. I just finished doing professional service in a psychiatric hospital. The hospital houses people with a range of mental disorders (Schizophrenia, Manic Depression, Bipolar Disorder, etc.). It also employs a multidisciplinary staff which includes social workers. It was very interesting to be able to see how a social worker performs within the mental health sector. It was also interesting to get to know the patients.

I have just asked to change institutions for my professional practice. I am now working in the DIF Municipal (Mexican Social Service Department) in Villa Garcia. I am actually living in Villa Garcia with my family right now and going back and forth to Aguascalientes for classes. It is a bit difficult because I have to wake up at 5:20am to ride the public transportation.

My family is doing well. I hope that you are also doing well. We have just celebrated the festival for the Virgin of Guadalupe. It was, as always, very beautiful. I don't have much time left of vacation.

I am doing well in school, but a bit worried about my course on law. It is very difficult and the professor does not explain it well. I have to study a lot for this class and I am praying that I don't fail. My next semester is my 7th and it is supposed to be the hardest. Pray for me.

Well, I am going to close for now. I will write again soon! My family sends their love.

My love,
Carla

Dear Sponsors,

Hello. I hope that this letter find you doing well and in the company of your family and friends. I am really glad to have this opportunity to write you and tell you how things are going in my life.

Here in Mexico we are all recovering from Christmas. December is a month of parties and celebrations and is full of family gatherings and food! It is a very special time for me and my family. We normally open our home to neighbors and friends for parties and gatherings to pray the rosary. Every year we make homemade candies to give away. On the 24-h of December we have the big celebration. We eat a large meal as a family and all of the little kids go to bed excited for el Niño Dios2.

On the 31 of December we normally go to Mass to thank God and the Virgin for all of the blessings they have given us throughout the year. After Mass we go back to our house, eat, and dance to welcome In the New Year. At midnight we make 12 wishes for each month of the year hoping that they all come true.

I am doing well in school. I am working hard to have good grades. My favorite class right now is chemistry. When we get back from break we will be making a model of the atomic structure of water. It should be very interesting.

Well, I hope that you had a very nice holiday. I also hope that all of your New Year wishes come true. Thank you for all of your support.

Sincerely,
Claudia

Dear Sponsor,

Hello! I hope that this letter finds you doing well. I also hope that you were able to spend a restful holiday with your family and loved ones. I am very grateful for the support and trust that you have given me. Because of you I am beginning to get closer to reaching my goal of being a professional. I do not want to let you or my parents down.

I am doing well in school. Some of the material from class is a review from high school, but for the most part I am learning a lot of new things. Even though the pace and atmosphere has been a very big change from high school.

College is great. I still do not know my final grades yet, but hope to have had good results.

My family is doing alright. My parents are a little worried because my dad lost his job in September. He has not found stable work yet and has been supporting us with small jobs that he finds. Even though his unemployment is a huge distress for us as a family it is also a time when we come together and feel closer than ever.

Well, I want to close by thanking you again for all of your support. Thank you so much. Take care. I look forward to writing the next time.

Sincerely,
Irene

Dear Sponsor,

First off, I want to send you a strong hug and warm Christmas greetings. I am happy to be able to write you all again and let you know what is going on in my life.

I had a really great semester. Actually, it was one of my best. I took a course called Geriatrics where I learned about the various sicknesses and health problems that affect the elderly. I really enjoyed the course and in the future I would very much like to work in the area of Geriatrics instead of my earlier choice, Cardiology.

I am also happy to tell you that I am working as an assistant in Villa Garcia's clinic. I really like the work and being able to apply what I am learning in school. I am learning so much from the experience. I see from 15-20 people a day. I work with patients with diabetes, hypertension, and respiratory problems. The majority of the patients are elderly. I really love working with them. I also feel that I am able to gain their trust. Working in the clinic with these particular patients has given me more motivation and desire to work within Geriatrics. The work is hard and I finish the day very tired. It is a good tired though. I read a quote once that said, "The day that you do not want to work, work in what you like the most and you will never have to work again."

Well, I am going to close for now. I hope that this 2011 will be a very happy one for you and your family. Thank you for all of your support.

Sincerely,
Bernardo

Hello dear sponsor,

I hope that my letter finds you enjoying good health. I also hope that you have had a wonderful holiday season.

I have been doing very well since the last time I wrote. I have completed my 7th semester in the university. I am very proud and happy because each semester is a challenge that I have accepted and overcome. This semester I took many interesting courses like, Cardiology and Oncology.

Next semester I will be taking a course on Geriatrics. I am looking forward to this class because I think that often times medicine puts more priority on young lives and I would like to learn how to care for the elderly. Although I believe young lives are important, I also think it is crucial that we care for our elders. I hope to be able to share some of the new things I learn about Geriatrics with you in my next letter.

I am still getting along very well with my classmates. Actually, we just had a female basketball tournament that was organized by the school of medicine. My team actually won!!! It was kind of funny because we were, for the most part, really bad at basketball. It was, honestly, thanks to one of our teammates, who is a really good player, that we won.

My family is doing really well. We had a wonderful Christmas. All of my brothers and sisters, their husbands and wives, and their children came to celebrate! It was great to see them, but a little overwhelming with all of the kids running around. ☺

Well, I am going to close for now. I hope that this 2011 will be a great one! Thank you, as always, for all of your support!

Sincerely,
Maria

Dear Sponsor,

Hello. First off, I want to tell you that I am very happy to be able to write again and let you know what is going on in my life. I hope that this letter finds you doing well. I also hope that you enjoyed your holidays.

Well, my grades are good and I am doing well in school. I had a little trouble with my English class last semester. The teacher was really strict and the final project was very hard for me. For our final project we had to prepare and give a presentation in English! It was very hard to be in front of the group speaking English. Mainly, my team and I felt nervous because the teacher was correcting our pronunciation.

My family is doing well. We were all together for Christmas. It was nice to be with my family, but I was also feeling sad. I have recently lost two very close friends.

I am looking forward to January when my cousins from Guadalajara will come to visit. I have not seen them for two years.

I am doing well at work. I am very close with the children I work with. I am especially close with a certain little boy. He is disabled, but has shown me that despite his disability he can still do many things. He is a very good example for me to follow.

Well, I will close for now. I hope that this 2011 will be a wonderful year for you and you family. Thank you, as always, for your support.

Sincerely,
Edith